LEISURE GUIDE

Devon

GW00587439

Author: Penny Phenix and Paul Murphy
Verifier: Sue Viccars
Managing Editor: David Popey
Project Management: Bookwork Creative Associates Ltd
Designers: Liz Baldin of Bookwork and Andrew Milne
Picture Library Manager: Ian Little
Picture Research: Liz Allen, Alice Earle, Carol Walker and Vivien Little
Cartography provided by the Mapping Services Department of AA Publishing
Copy-editors: Marilynne Lanng of Bookwork and Pamela Stagg
Internal Repro and Image Reproduction: Jacqueline Street
Production: Rachel Davis

Produced by AA Publishing
© AA Media Limited 2007
Reprinted 2007, 2008
Updated and revised 2010

Published by AA Publishing (a trading name of AA Media Limited, whose registered office is Fanum House, Basing View, Basingstoke, Hampshire RG21 4EA; registered number 06112600).

This product includes mapping data licensed from the Ordnance Survey® with the permission of the Controller of Her Majesty's Stationery Office. © Crown Copyright 2011. All rights reserved. Licence number 100021153.

ISBN 978-0-7495-6686-9
ISBN 978-0-7495-6699-9 (SS)

A CIP catalogue record for this book is available from the British Library.

CONTENTS

Welcome to...

Devon

It's easy to work out why Devon is such a popular tourist destination. This beautiful county offers so much: a sunny climate, fabulous beaches, great industrial heritage, a wealth of wildlife and a variety of landscapes. Devon has sweeping moorland, wooded valleys, patchwork farmland, wildfowl-rich wetland, broad estuaries, sparkling rivers and a superb coastline.

Devon can be divided into five areas: Exmoor and the north coast, the rural heart of the county, Dartmoor and the Tamar valley, the south coast which includes the South Hams, and Exeter and the east of the county.

Exmoor – moorland, wooded combes, small hedged fields, ancient farms and villages – straddles the Devon–Somerset border (two thirds falls in Somerset). The area's main attractions are the stunning coastline and soaring cliffs. There are few sandy beaches, but glorious expanses can be found to the west at Woolacombe and Saunton Sands. Further west still, past Bideford, lies Devon's remotest corner, Hartland Point.

Moving south into Devon's heartland is like taking a step back in time. Remote hamlets untouched by the effects of tourism, mile upon mile of narrow-hedged lanes, old market towns, fabulous pubs and the feel of 'real' Devon. This is authentic Tarka Country, crossed by the popular cycle trail and renowned for salmon fishing on the great rivers Taw and Torridge.

Next comes Dartmoor, a tougher, bleaker moorland, with weathered granite tors, Bronze Age stone circles and plentiful tin-working remains. Dartmoor's moorland streams have carved deep valleys at the granite edge, providing opportunities for walks and picnics. The beautiful River Tamar meets the sea at the lively city of Plymouth, still a significant port.

South Devon is almost like a different country, renowned for its balmy climate. This is Devon's main tourist area, with thousands filling the resort of Torbay. But a couple of miles away are quiet villages of cob and thatch cottages, flower-filled lanes and the South Hams coastline. Watersports abound at Salcombe and Dartmouth, and there are wonderful secluded coves. Finally to historic Exeter – the county town – and the east. Here the famous red soils outcrop on hills and vales, and on the cliffs at Budleigh Salterton and Sidmouth. East Devon has a civilised air, lent by its popularity as a holiday destination since Regency times.

WALES

Lundy

Burnham-
on-Sea

Highbridge

Bridgwater

Taunton

Wellington

Ilminster

Chard

**EXMOOR &
NORTH COAST**

Lynton

1

Ilfracombe

1

Braunton

Barnstaple

Hartland
Point

1 Clovelly

Northam

Bideford

South Molton

Great
Torringon

**DEVON'S RURAL
HEARTLAND**

Tiverton

2

Bickleigh

2

9 Broadhembury

Honiton

Crediton

**EXETER &
EAST DEVON**

Okehampton

2

Bridford

4

Exeter

Sidmouth

10 Branscombe

Lyme
Regis

Tavistock

3

Princetown

3

**DARTMOOR
& TAMAR
VALLEY**

Bovey
Tracey

5

Exmouth

Teignmouth

Newton
Abbot

Torquay

Plympton

Totnes

Paignton

**SOUTH
COAST**

Brixham

Plymouth

Dartmouth

8

Saltash

6

Kingsbridge

Bigbury-
on-Sea

Salcombe

7

Bude

Launceston

Liskeard

Torpoint

6	Walk start point
1	Cycle start point
2	Tour start point

ESSENTIAL SIGHTS

Beaches, rugged moorland, cute villages with cob and thatch cottages and cobbled streets, wildlife, outdoor sports from sailing to climbing – Devon has got them all. For 3 miles (4.8km) of golden sandy beach and the chance to go surfing, but not necessarily peace and tranquillity, head to Saunton Sands; for challenging walking and rock climbing, head to Dartmoor, one of England's few remaining wildernesses; and for classic holiday resort fun try Torbay. For walking with fantastic sea views (and easy navigation), there's the South West Coast Path and for a dedicated cycle path, there are 180 miles (290km) of it on the Tarka Trail. In terms of things to go and see, visit Bickleigh Castle, Buckfast Abbey, A La Ronde or Arlington Court.

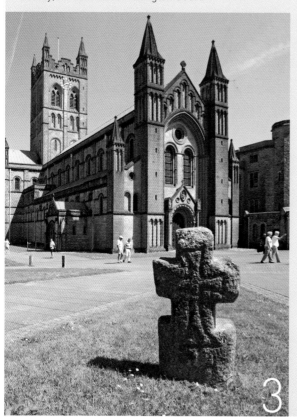

1 Hope Cove

The delightful cove, near the fishing village of the same name, is known for its fantastic crabs and lobsters. Once it was the haunt of smugglers and the craggy coastline saw several shipwrecks, but now it is a lure for visitors who come here to sail, dive or relax and look at the tranquil view.

2 Saunton Sands

The sea off Saunton Sands is popular with surfers, while the beach attracts families. Braunton Burrows just inland is where marram grass anchors the shifting sands. The safest part of the beach is to the north, while the further south you go, the likelier you are to find an emptier more peaceful place to relax.

3 Buckfast Abbey

A community of Benedictine monks lives, works and worships here. You can tour the extensive estate, and see the beehives and winery for which the abbey is famous, as well as buy honey and Buckfast Tonic Wine.

4 Porlock Bay
The shingle ridge at Porlock bay stretches for around a mile (1.6km).

5 Dartmoor National Park
Ponies have been grazing Dartmoor for centuries, although most of those you see today are cross-breeds.

6 Woolacombe
This is a charming holiday town, popular with families, who come for the sandy blue-flag beach, and surfers, who come to ride the waves.

7 Hay Tor
The most-visited tor in the National Park also offers some of the best climbing in the area.

8 Hartland's coast
When the sea is tranquil the views from the quay stretch as far as Lundy. However, when storms rage, the sea churns spectacularly against the rocks.

9 Beer
The high cliffs above the beach form a natural windbreak. Beer and its shingle beach are perfect for a relaxing holiday.

4

5

6

DAY ONE

For many people a weekend break or a long weekend is a popular way of spending their leisure time. The next four pages offer a loosely planned itinerary designed to ensure that you make the most of your time and enjoy the very best the area has to offer. Options for each part of the weekend as well as wet-weather alternatives are suggested.

Friday Night

Stay at the wonderful Horn of Plenty at Gulworthy (3 miles/4.8km west of Tavistock on the A390). It's a country house hotel and award-winning restaurant with fantastic views across the Tamar valley to Bodmin Moor. Have your pre-dinner drinks before a blazing log fire in the winter, or in the garden under a vine-covered pergola during the warmer summer months.

Saturday Morning

Begin by driving south via the B3257 to Morwellham Quay, a fascinating re-creation of a copper port in its heyday, and part of the Cornwall and West Devon Mining World Heritage Site, designated in 2006.

The highlight of a visit is a trip on the old miners' railway, which takes you deep underground into one of the mines, where vivid tableaux and a commentary illustrate the life of the workers there. Above ground again, don't miss a stroll around the farmyard and the stables of the shire horses.

Saturday Lunch

Drive up through Tavistock and on to Dartmoor to the Peter Tavy Inn at Peter Tavy. The pub, which is fully restored complete with old flagstone floors and oak timbers, combines good food with views of the moor.

Wet-weather option

If it's raining spend the day in Plymouth and get undercover in the National Marine Aquarium or the Plymouth Gin Distillery.

Saturday Afternoon

Drive northwest to walk off your lunch in the spectacular Lydford Gorge. Marvel at the dramatic Devil's Cauldron, close to Lydford Bridge, and the White Lady Waterfall, 90-feet (27m) high, at the end of the gorge. There are paths of various lengths, but the full walk runs to about 3.5 miles (5.6km).

Saturday Night

Loop around the top of Dartmoor (no roads cross the wild northwestern part), then down through narrow lanes to spend the night at the Gidleigh Park Hotel, near Chagford – not for those travelling on a budget.

WHITE LADY WATERFALL, LYDFORD GORGE

DAY TWO

Though it may be hard to tear yourself away from such a fine hotel, this is the day to explore the delightful little villages and lanes of eastern Dartmoor en route to one of the most impressive religious foundations in the country. After that, take a scenic boat trip between two of Devon's most interesting old towns.

Sunday Morning

Drive through the famous villages of Widecombe in the Moor and Buckland in the Moor before continuing southwards to Buckfastleigh. Buckfast Abbey is the main attraction here, with its beautiful abbey church, constructed in the early part of the 20th century and surely worth visiting for the stained glass alone. The monks here have become famous for their Buckfast Tonic Wine and for the honey from the Buckfast hives, so allow time to visit their shop before you leave.

Buckfastleigh is also the home of Dartmoor Otters and Buckfast Butterflies. The butterfly farm is particularly delightful on a chilly day because the glasshouses are kept at a tropical temperature. Both of these attractions are just behind the station, which is the terminus of the South Devon Railway where steam trains run for 7 scenic miles (11.3km) along the Dart Valley (check return times).

Sunday Lunch

Stop for lunch at The Waterman's Arms at Ashprington. This famous country inn has an interesting past – it has been a smithy and a brewhouse and was even a prison during the Napoleonic Wars.

Situated on the banks of the River Cart next to the Bow Bridge, the inn is full of character. The bars have exposed beams and open fires and there's an extensive snack menu with tempting daily specials. The informal restaurant is separate.

Sunday Afternoon

Take a boat trip down the beautiful River Dart from Totnes to Dartmouth and back. You will pass Greenway house on the way – the place where Agatha Christie wrote many of her novels.

Dartmouth's network of tiny cobbled streets are delightful to explore and are a good place to indulge in a bout of window-shopping among the galleries, craft shops and boutiques. The historic quay at Bayard's Cove has hardly changed since the days of sail.

Totnes has a Norman castle, some well-preserved buildings, more craft shops and galleries and one of the most attractive high streets in the country.

Wet-weather option

Go to Exeter to see the cathedral, then visit the city's Royal Albert Memorial Museum. The Underground Passages are protected from the elements.

INFORMATION

Route facts

MINIMUM TIME The time stated for completing each route is the estimated minimum time that a reasonably fit family group of walkers or cyclists would take to complete the circuit. This does not allow for rest or refreshment stops.

OS MAP Each route is shown on a map. However, some detail is lost because of the restrictions imposed by scale, so for this reason, we recommend that you use the maps in conjunction with a more detailed Ordnance Survey map. The relevant map for each walk or cycle ride is listed.

START This indicates the start location and parking area. This is a six-figure grid reference prefixed by two letters showing which 62.5-mile (100km) square of the National Grid it refers to. You'll find more information on grid references on most Ordnance Survey maps.

CYCLE HIRE We list, within reason, the nearest cycle hire shop/centre.

❶ Here we highlight any potential difficulties or dangers along the cycle ride or walk. If a particular route is suitable for older, fitter children we say so here. Also, we give guidelines of a route's suitability for younger children, for example the symbol 8+ indicates that the route can probably be attempted by children aged 8 years and above.

Walks & Cycle Rides

Each walk and cycle ride has a panel giving information for the walker and cyclist, including the distance, terrain, nature of the paths, and where to park your car.

WALKING

All of the walks are suitable for families, but less experienced family groups, especially those with younger children, should try the shorter walks. Route finding is usually straightforward, but the maps are for guidance only and we recommend that you always take the relevant Ordnance Survey map with you.

Risks

Although each walk has been researched with a view to minimising any risks, no walk in the countryside can be considered to be completely free from risk. Walking in the outdoors will always require a degree of common sense and judgement to ensure that it is as safe as possible, especially for young children.

• Be particularly careful on cliff paths and in upland terrain, where the consequences of a slip can be serious.

• Remember to check tidal conditions before walking on the seashore.

• Some sections of route are by, or cross, busy roads.

Remember traffic is a danger even on minor country lanes.

• Be careful around farmyard machinery and livestock.

• Be prepared for the consequences of changes in the weather and check the forecast before you set out.

• Ensure the whole family is properly equipped, wearing suitable clothing and a good pair of boots or sturdy walking shoes. Take waterproof clothing with you and a torch if you are walking in the winter months.

• Remember the weather can change quickly at any time of the year, and in moorland and heathland areas, mist and fog can make route-finding much harder. In summer, take account of the heat and sun by wearing a hat, sunscreen and carrying enough water.

• On walks away from centres of population you should carry a mobile phone, whistle and, if possible, a survival bag. If you do have an accident requiring emergency services, make a note of your position as accurately as possible and dial 999 (112 on a mobile).

CYCLING

In devising the cycle rides in this guide, every effort has been made to use designated cycle paths, or to link them with quiet country lanes and waymarked byways and bridleways. In a few cases, some fairly busy B-roads have been used to join up with quieter routes.

Rules of the road

- Ride in single file on narrow and busy roads.
- Be alert, look and listen for traffic, especially on narrow lanes and blind bends and be extra careful when descending steep hills, as loose gravel or a poor road surface can lead to an accident.
- In wet weather make sure that you keep an appropriate distance between you and other riders.
- Make sure you indicate your intentions clearly.
- Brush up on *The Highway Code* before venturing out onto the road.

Off-road safety code of conduct

- Only ride where you know it is legal to do so. Cyclists are not allowed to cycle on public footpaths (yellow waymarks). The only 'rights of way' open to cyclists are bridleways (blue markers) and unsurfaced tracks, known as byways, which are open to all traffic and waymarked in red.
- Canal tow paths: you need a permit to cycle on some stretches of tow path (www. waterscape.com). Remember that access paths can be steep and slippery so always push your bike under low bridges and by locks.
- Always yield to walkers and horses, giving adequate warning of your approach.
- Don't expect to cycle at high speeds.
- Keep to the main trail to avoid any unnecessary erosion to the area beside the trail and to prevent skidding, especially in wet weather conditions.
- Remember to follow the Country Code.

Preparing your bicycle

Check the wheels, tyres, brakes and cables. Lubricate hubs, pedals, gear mechanisms and cables. Make sure you have a pump, a bell, a rear rack to carry panniers and a set of lights.

Equipment

- A cycling helmet provides essential protection.
- Make sure you are visible to other road users, by wearing light-coloured or luminous clothing in daylight and sashes or reflective strips in failing light and darkness.
- Take extra clothes with you, depending on the season, and a wind/waterproof jacket.
- Carry a basic tool kit, a pump, a strong lock and a first aid kit.
- Always carry enough water for your outing.

Walk Map Legend

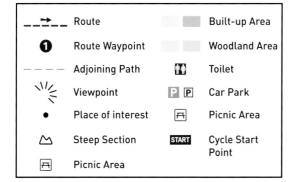

___→___	Route		Built-up Area
❶	Route Waypoint		Woodland Area
– – – –	Adjoining Path	🚻	Toilet
☼	Viewpoint	P P	Car Park
●	Place of interest	🎪	Picnic Area
△	Steep Section	START	Cycle Start Point
🎪	Picnic Area		

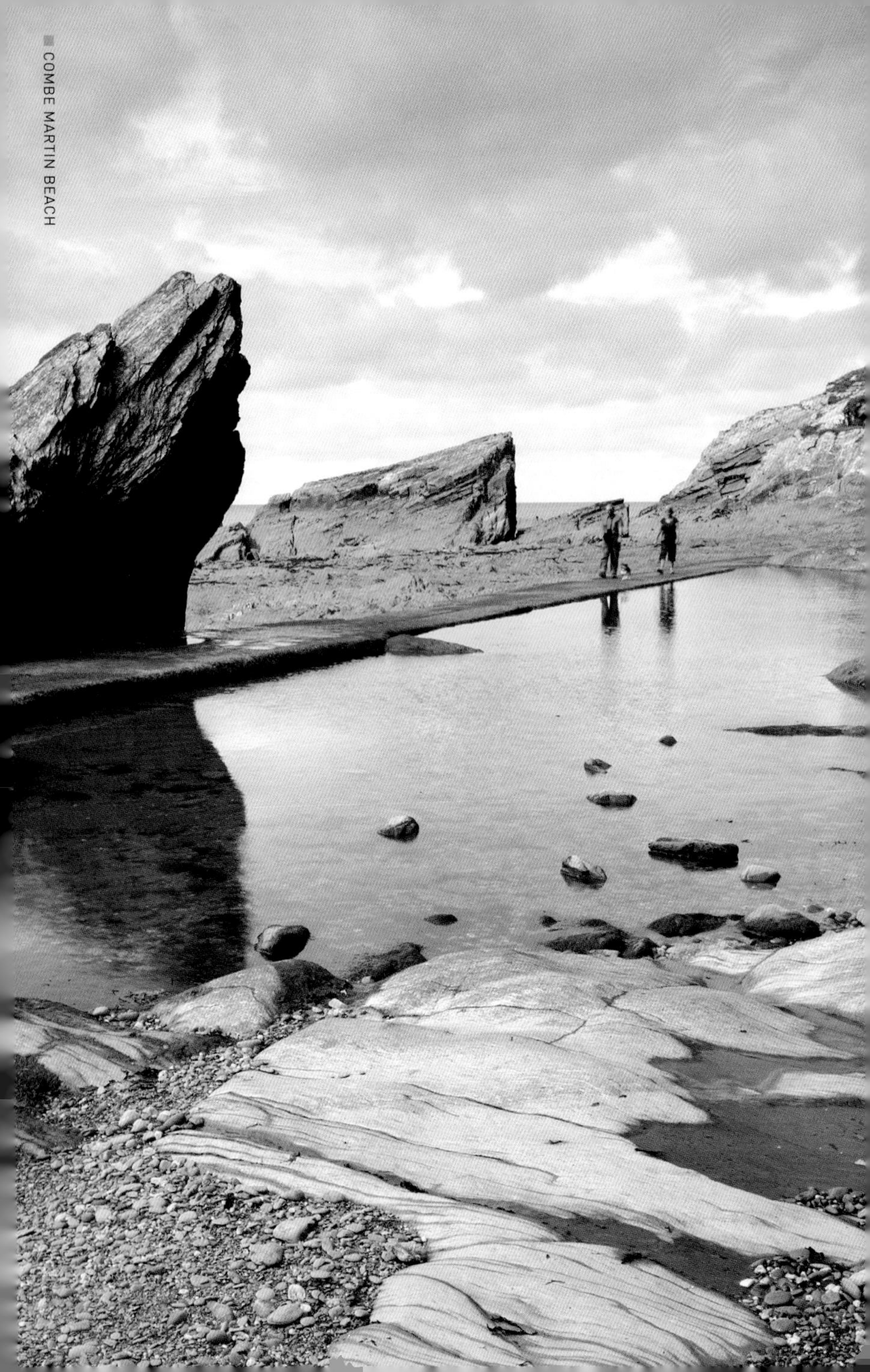

COMBE MARTIN BEACH

Exmoor & North Coast

The north coast of Devon encompasses many changes in character from east to west. At its most easterly point, it is backed by Exmoor, with deep combes cutting their way down to the sea between steeply folded wooded slopes. West of the national park are the traditional holiday resorts of Ilfracombe and Woolacombe and a series of long sandy beaches. Beyond Barnstaple and Bideford it changes again, with rocky foreshores that have to be approached steeply from above and delightful villages, such as Bucks Mills and Clovelly, perched above their harbours. The rocks continue around Hartland Point down to the lovely Welcombe beach.

WATERSMEET

SAUNTON SANDS

Porlock Weir
A39
Minehead
EXMOOR
Dunster
NATIONAL
Wheddon Cross
B3224
PARK
B3223
A396
SOMERSET
Dulverton
A361
Wellington
A38

1	Walk start point
1	Cycle start point
1	Tour start point

A361
Tiverton

HARTLAND QUAY

Unmissable attractions

To appreciate this region fully, try to visit Exmoor National Park as well as a beach or two to the west. For (literally) miles of golden sandy beach, pack your picnic and surf board and head to Saunton Sands. Walking boots and binoculars are what you'll need to best appreciate the stretch of the South West Coast Path, which takes you to dramatic Hartland Point. Unmissable places in Exmoor National Park include the classic, National Trust-managed beauty spot of Watersmeet, the sight of hardy Exmoor ponies and lovely little villages like Selworthy.

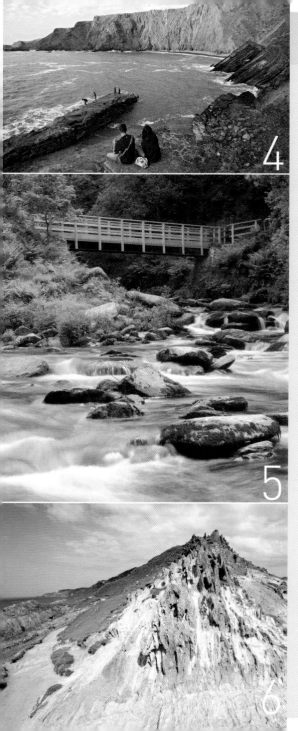

1 Exmoor National Park coastline

This beautiful coastline at the edge of the national park is the perfect place for a bracing walk.

2 Appledore

Pretty Appledore has narrow alleys, fishermen's cottages and craft shops and galleries. At low tide tethered boats sit patiently beached on the sand.

3 The Valley of Rocks

A path leads from Lynton to this stunning viewpoint, a popular place with rock climbers.

4 Hartland Quay

The South West Coast Path runs from Somerset right round to Dorset. The stretch from Hartland Point to Hartland Quay is 3 miles (4.8km) past dramatic cliffs and the lighthouse.

5 Watersmeet

Watersmeet is an Area of Outstanding Natural Beauty. Near Lynmouth, it is where the West Lyn River and Hoaroak Water meet.

6 Morte Point

This dramatic spot near Woolacombe is just part of an Area of Outstanding Natural Beauty and is a favourite with walkers. From Morte Point you can see the whole of the north Devon coast.

APPLEDORE MAP REF SS4630

Appledore's narrow cobbled streets, only just wide enough for a single car and lined with pretty colour-washed cottages, rise steeply up the hillside from the quay on the Torridge estuary. But, delightful though it certainly is, this is not simply a tourist village living on its appearance. Appledore is a lively community with a strong sense of its ancient maritime traditions. Sadly, although shipbuilding and seafaring have occupied the workforce since medieval times, the famous shipyard has now closed down.

Appropriately, Appledore is the home of the North Devon Maritime Museum, set in a listed building overlooking the village. Each room shows a different aspect of the maritime activities of the area, and there is a reconstruction of an Appledore kitchen at around the turn of the century. Visit the museum and then stroll around the village and along the quay to really soak up the atmosphere of the place.

ARLINGTON COURT

MAP REF SS6140

There is no getting away from the fact that the exterior of Arlington Court is fine, but rather austere. Indeed, it is plain, but don't judge this particular book by its cover, for inside is a series of rooms that are beautifully designed and furnished and that house a number of wonderful collections. Generations of the Chichester family have lived at Arlington, but today it reflects most of all the character of the last of them to live there – the remarkable and immensely energetic Miss Rosalie Chichester, who kindly bequeathed her home to the National Trust when she died in 1949.

An intrepid traveller and compulsive collector, Miss Chichester filled the house with collections, including 200 ship models, 75 cabinets full of shells, hundreds of pieces of pewter and snuff boxes and items collected during her world travels. One of the nicest things about Arlington Court is the lack of barriers, which means that visitors can wander at will around each of the rooms and inspect the contents close up.

A pleasant walk through the grounds leads to the superb stable block, which is a major attraction in itself. This is where the National Trust's collection of nearly 50 horse-drawn vehicles is kept, from enormous state carriages to a delightful little carriage built for a child in true fairy-tale fashion.

BARNSTAPLE MAP REF SS5633

Pay a flying visit to Barnstaple and you may be forgiven for thinking that it is a town much like any other. Its main shopping streets, partly pedestrianised, have the kinds of stores you will see in any high street along with a modern shopping mall, but you will be well rewarded if you explore, for there are attractive little alleyways, quiet corners and some fine buildings. These include the covered Pannier Market, built in the mid-19th century, where traditional markets as well as craft and antiques markets are held. Part of the same development is Butcher's Row, built to house 33 butchers' shops, though it has now been infiltrated by greengrocers, fishmongers and delicatessens.

One of the most historic sites in Barnstaple is the huge mound created by the Normans as a vantage point for their castle (only fragments of the original wall remain). But Barnstaple's history goes back further; records show that it was already the commercial centre for north Devon when it was first granted a charter in AD 930. It continued to prosper, becoming a major port for trade with America, and the ornate Queen Anne's Building down by the river dates from that era. Extensively renovated, it is now open to the public and contains the excellent Barnstaple Heritage Centre, portraying the history of the town with interactive displays and 'face-to-face' speaking models of figures from the town's past. These include the Elizabethan town clerk Adam Wyatt, whose book *Lost Chronicle* is on sale in the Heritage Centre shop,

■ **Insight**

BARNSTAPLE FAIR

This event has its origins far back in history and is probably as old as the town itself. Beginning on the Wednesday before 20 September, the festivities once followed on from the great annual market, but are now purely for entertainment and ceremony. The fair begins with the Town Council gathering in the Guildhall to make toasts with a traditional spiced ale. At midday a proclamation is read out, then this is repeated at the southern end of the High Street and on the Strand. On the Saturday there is a carnival, with decorated floats that raise money for local charities.

and Mistress Grace Beaple, who, during the Civil War, sheltered Prince Charles (later Charles II). There are also fine reconstructions of the interior of a merchant's ship, a Civil War trench and scenes from earlier eras in the town.

Near the bridge the Museum of North Devon has lively and imaginative exhibits, including a room which takes visitors into an underwater world, complete with sound effects, with giant turtles and large fish mounted on a realistic marine background. The display of north Devon pottery is spectacular and, of course, Tarka the Otter is never very far away (the Tarka Trail passes through the town).

A little way north of the town are the famous Marwood Hill Gardens, which occupy about 20 acres (8ha) of a sheltered valley. Pathways lead down between the hillside trees and shrubs to a series of lakes, inhabited by some enormous koi carp.

BIDEFORD MAP REF SS4526

Bideford is a lovely little town with enormous character. Its focal point is the quay, which was built in the 17th century and was a hive of activity in the town's seafaring heyday, when Bideford men were renowned for their nautical skills. Those days are long gone, but there are always a few coasters tied up alongside to keep alive something of the town's tradition. They share the waters with pleasure craft, including the boat for Lundy. The Torridge river is spanned here by an ancient 24-arch stone bridge, but increasing traffic in the last few decades was seriously weakening it, and a new bridge and bypass now cross high over the estuary downstream – the views from it are wonderful.

From the quay, a network of narrow streets and alleyways (called 'drangs') climbs the hillside, lined with good butcher, baker and greengrocer shops alongside craft shops, art galleries, antiques and junk shops – the traffic-free parts are particularly pleasant. A steep climb leads up to the Pannier Market, built in 1884, though the market has been held since 1272. The Burton Museum and Art Gallery hosts a wide variety of events, and features the work of local craftspeople.

Standing just west of Bideford, near Abbotsham, is the Big Sheep, part of a large working sheep farm, which is interesting and informative, with sheep milking, shearing, lamb-feeding, sheepdog trials and spinning, but the abiding memory which most visitors take home with them is of the hilarious sheep racing.

CLOVELLY MAP REF SS3124

Of all Devon's pretty villages, this must surely be the most famous and the most visited – which can make it too crowded for comfort at the height of the season. You need real stamina to visit Clovelly. Its single cobbled street has an alarming gradient which drops some 400 feet (122m) over the course of half a mile, and traffic is banned, so visitors have to park at the top of the hill and explore on foot. Two things you should be aware of: first, because of the steep cobbles, wear sensible footwear; second, visitors enter the village through the visitor centre and pay an admission fee. But if all this strikes you as commercialised, don't be put off, because Clovelly is well worth it. As if the narrow cobbled street weren't picturesque enough, the delightful colour-washed 16th-century cottages that cluster along its slopes are decked with flowers and shrubs, and at the bottom is the lovely little harbour.

If you find walking back up the street a trial, spare a thought for those who live here – everything, from food to fuel and furniture, has to be carried down this street, or lowered on sleds. A word of comfort for those who may be weak of leg and short of breath – there is a Land Rover service from Easter to October to the car park by a back route.

On the way to Clovelly along the A39 near Bucks Mills is Hobby Drive. It was constructed as a hobby (hence the name) in the 19th century by a wealthy local landowner, Sir James Hamlyn Williams. It is closed to traffic now, but offers a 3-mile (4.8km) walk through wooded slopes above the coastline.

From Brownsham to Clovelly

A walk along the coastal path to the picturesque village of Clovelly, which clings to the wooded cliffs on the long, virtually uninhabited stretch of coastline between Bideford and Hartland Point. The return leg passes through farmland and forest.

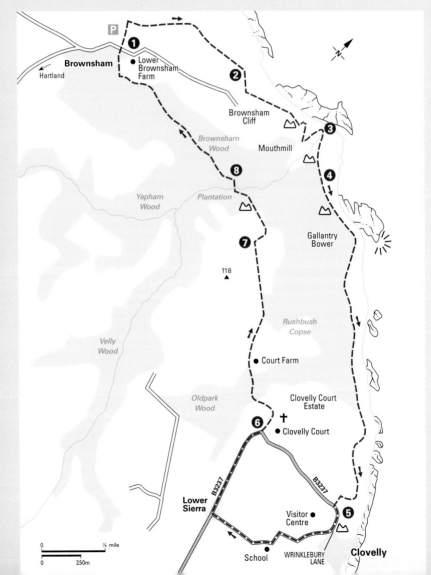

Route Directions

1 Follow the footpath from the back of the car park, signed 'Buckland Woods'. Pass through a gate into woods. Follow signs 'Footpath to coast path' to pass a bench at a path junction. Go straight on to cross over a stile and on to meet the coast path.

2 Go right over a stile (signed 'Mouthmill') into the field on Brownsham Cliff. There are good views ahead to Morte Point. Keep to the left edge, across a stile, down steps and left round the next field. Cross a stile and zig-zag downhill through woodland. When you leave the trees turn left towards the sea at Mouthmill (note the lime kiln).

3 Follow the coast path across the rocky beach. Clamber up a rocky gully to meet a track on a bend; walk uphill (left).

4 Eventually follow coast path signs left, then immediately right. Go left up wooden steps to follow a narrow, wooded path uphill towards the open cliff top at Gallantry Bower, with a 400ft (122m) drop into the sea. Re-enter woodland and follow the signed path to pass 'the Angel's Wings' folly. Where a path leads straight on to the church, keep left following signs and later via a gate through the edge of Clovelly Court estate. Enter laurel woods via a kissing gate. The path winds down and up past a stone shelter, then through a kissing gate into a field. Keep to the left; through a gate and oak trees to meet the road at a big gate. Follow coast path signs on to the road that leads to the top of Clovelly village below the Visitor Centre.

5 Leave the coast path and walk up deep, steep, ancient Wrinkleberry Lane (right of Hobby Drive ahead) to a lane, past the school and on to meet the road. Turn right.

6 Where the road bends right go through the gates to Clovelly Court. By the church (right) follow bridleway signs left ('Court Farm & sawmills') through the farm. At the end of buildings keep ahead on a track between fields. Pass through a plantation, then bear right downhill across a field as signed.

7 Go through a gate (by a bridlepath sign). At the bottom of the field go through a gate into a plantation, downhill.

8 Turn left at the forest track, following bridleway signs. Turn right as signed to cross the stream and up the long, gradually ascending track to Lower Brownsham Farm. Turn left for the car park.

Route facts

DISTANCE/TIME 5.25 miles (8.4 km) 2h15

MAP OS Explorer 126 Clovelly & Hartland

START National Trust car park at Brownsham, grid ref: SS 282260

TRACKS Grassy coast path, woodland and farm tracks, 4 stiles

GETTING TO THE START
From the A39 just west of Clovelly Cross roundabout, take the B3248, signed for Hartland. In a mile (1.6km) fork right towards Hartland lighthouse. Take the next right at Highdown Cross towards Brownsham. Fork right again and drive past the National Trust buildings on the right. The car park is marked on the left.

THE PUB The Red Lion, Clovelly. Tel: 01237 431237; www.clovelly.co.uk

❶ Undulating coast – some steep climbs.

From Braunton to Barnstaple

A gentle linear ride along the Tarka Trail from historic Braunton to Barnstaple's old quayside. As you set off look right to the ridge of Braunton Burrows – the second largest dune system in the UK.

Route Directions

1 The car park marks the site of the old Braunton railway station, closed in 1965. The line – Barnstaple to Ilfracombe – was opened in 1874, and the last train ran in 1970. Cycle to the far end of the car park and turn right into the overflow area. Bear left and leave the car park by the police station (right). Bear right onto Station Road and cycle down it, passing the cycle hire on the left. Turn right into Station Close and then immediately left down a tarmac way. At the end cross the lane; keep ahead through black bollards to cross another lane, with a roundabout right.

2 Follow signs left to pick up the old railway line. Pass a conservation area (left) and pass round a staggered barrier to cross a lane (wire fences on the right mark the boundary of RAF Chivenor).

3 (Note: For the Williams Arms turn left here; at the end of the lane cross the A361 with care.) Cycle on to reach a roundabout at the entrance to RAF Chivenor. The church ahead left is St Augustine's at Heanton Punchardon, which was built by Richard Punchardon (owner of Heanton estate) after his return from the Crusades in the 13th century. The village, formerly Heanton, took his name from that time. Cross the road by the roundabout and keep ahead through a wooded section.

4 Emerge suddenly from woodland onto the Taw estuary, with far-reaching views. Stop to listen for the oystercatcher's piping call, and watch out for curlew, identified by its curving bill. In winter thousands of migrant birds feed here on the broad sandbanks. Pass the Tarka Inn (formerly Heanton Court), a refuge for Royalists in the Civil War. The then owner of the Heanton estate, Colonel Albert Basset, fought for Barnstaple, which fell to the Parliamentarians. Continue along the Taw to pass the football club (left).

5 Cross arched Yeo Bridge, a swing bridge over a tributary of the Taw, and pass the Civic Centre on the left (cyclists and pedestrians separate here). Bear left away from the river to meet the road. Turn right along the cycle path past old Barnstaple Town Station on the right. Bear right as signed, then left along the

Route facts

DISTANCE/TIME 11 miles (17.6km) 1h30

MAP OS Explorer 139 Bideford, Ilfracombe & Barnstaple

START Braunton car park (contributions), grid ref: SS 486365

TRACKS Level tarmac and gritty former railway track

GETTING TO THE START Braunton lies on the A361 Barnstaple to Ilfracombe road. The car park is signed from the traffic lights in the centre of the village. If approaching from Barnstaple, turn left and 100yds (91m) later turn left into the car park.

CYCLE HIRE Otter Cycle Hire, Braunton, tel: 01271 813339 or Tarka Trail Cycle Hire, Barnstaple, tel: 01271 324202; www.tarkabikes.co.uk

THE PUB The Williams Arms, Wrafton. Tel: 01271 812360; www.williamsarms.co.uk

❶ Busy crossing of A361 on route to the Williams Arms.

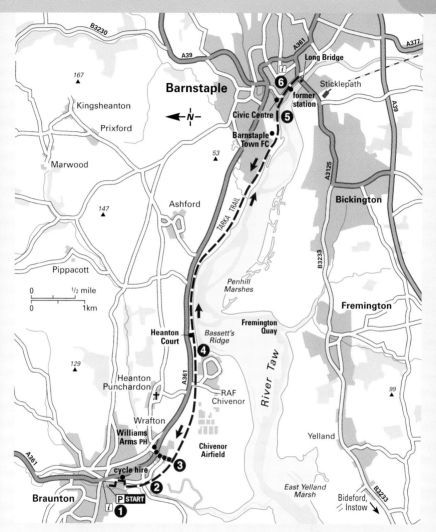

quay (note: take care as there is no wall along the edge).

6 Continue on to pass Barnstaple Heritage Centre (left), with its elaborate statue of Queen Anne. The Riverside Café (with cycle racks) lies a few yards along on the left, just before Barnstaple's Long Bridge over the Taw (there has been a bridge here since the 13th century). There is evidence of a settlement at Barnstaple from Saxon times; trade via the Taw was vital to the town's prosperity for centuries. Queen Anne's Walk marks the site of the Great and Little Quays, once bustling with ocean-going ships, including five bound for Sir Francis Drake's Armada fleet in 1588.

COMBE MARTIN   MAP REF SS5846

Combe Martin is said to be the largest village in Devon, and, as it is strung out along a narrow valley, its other claim to fame is having the longest main street (about 2 miles/3.2km) of any village in the country. The late 17th-century Pack O'Cards pub stands out among the otherwise standard seaside village architecture. Its construction was financed by the winnings from a card game, so it was built with four storeys to represent the four suits in a pack; each floor has 13 doors, for the cards in each suit, and there are 52 windows, one for each card in the pack.

Though Combe Martin may not be one of the prettiest places, it does meet the sea at a nice little rocky bay with a sandy beach and plenty of rock pools at low tide. The nearby Combe Martin Wildlife and Dinosaur Park is set among woodland with clear streams, cascading waterfalls and beautiful ornamental gardens. Its inhabitants include otters and the delightful meerkats, which have as their home the largest enclosure

Insight

HUNTING THE EARL

If you are in Combe Martin over the Spring Bank Holiday, you will witness the Hunting of the Earl of Rone, a ceremony with its roots in pagan times but which has been adapted over the centuries to incorporate other historical events. The original Hobby Horse procession is now preceded by a chase through the woods in pursuit of the 'Earl', who is then placed backwards on a donkey and led in the main procession to the beach, where he is unceremoniously dumped in the sea.

(a man-made desert) in Europe. On the road to Ilfracombe, Watermouth Castle is great fun for children, with attractions from adventure playgrounds to fairy-tale tableaux to antique penny-in-the-slot machines and 'dancing water' shows.

DUNSTER   MAP REF SS9943

On the eastern edge of Exmoor and actually in Somerset, Dunster is one of the most picturesque medieval villages in the country, complete with a huge Norman castle that dominates the entire area. Now in the care of the National Trust, Dunster Castle was substantially altered in the early 17th century and further work was carried out in 1868, but its core medieval character was preserved to a large extent. The oak-panelled halls have magnificent ceilings and there are many reminders of the Luttrell family, who called this home for some 600 years until 1950.

The village is one of the loveliest in Britain, its medieval character perfectly preserved. The main street of pretty little shops and tearooms sits cosily between two high wooded hills, one topped by the castle, and is distinguished by the octagonal Yarn Market, a relic of its days as an important wool centre.

EXMOOR

Exmoor, on the border of Devon and Somerset, has some wonderful and varied scenery. On the coast between Combe Martin and Countisbury, rivers that rise on the open moorland have cut deep ravines, meeting the sea between enormous rock faces that climb almost vertically from the water, forming some of the highest cliffs in Britain. Further inland is the high moorland plateau, with deep wooded valleys and charming, picturesque villages such as Winsford, Selworthy and Allerford.

The 267-square mile (691sq km) National Park was established in 1954 to preserve a unique and beautiful landscape, but most of it remains in private ownership and so continues to be farmed. However, visitors to the area enjoy considerable freedom to explore the countryside, and the best way to do this is on foot or on horseback. Some of the best woodland walks can be found around Dulverton, Dunster and Cloutsham, and on the coast path. About 12,000 acres (4,860ha) of the moor are owned and conserved by the National Trust, including Watersmeet, the park's most famous beauty spot.

Britain's largest wild animal, the red deer, survives on Exmoor, but easier to see are the sturdy little Exmoor ponies that roam the moor, believed to be descended from the prehistoric wild horse. Overhead, the sight of buzzards effortlessly soaring is not uncommon, and you may also catch sight of fulmars and oystercatchers along the coast.

One way to be sure of seeing a large variety of birds and animals is to visit the delightful Exmoor Zoological Park at South Stowford, 12 acres (5ha) of landscaped gardens and informal paddocks in lovely countryside.

For an introduction to Exmoor as a whole, pay a visit to one of the excellent museums – the Lyn and Exmoor Museum at Lynton and Allerford's West Somerset Rural Life Museum are particularly good.

Insight

LORNA DOONE
The deep combes and heather-clad moorland around Malmsmead and Oare are the setting for R. D. Blackmore's famous story of the tragic heroine Lorna Doone and her lawless family. It is based on the exploits of a real family of Scottish outlaws who came to Exmoor, failed at farming and turned instead to a life of crime. 'Doone Valley' is now the focus of walking, horse-riding and car tours.

HARTLAND POINT
MAP REF SS2524

To many people, Hartland Point is more dramatic than Land's End. It looks out over one of the most treacherous stretches of water in Britain, with strong currents and huge jagged rocks. Even on the calmest of days, the waters swirl menacingly around the headland, and in a storm the crashing waves are truly spectacular. Just to the east is lovely, unspoiled Shipload Bay (National Trust), practically inaccessible since the steps leading to the beach were damaged. Hartland Quay is 3 miles (4.8km) in the other direction, but you don't have to walk – there is good access by road and plenty of parking, especially at the lowest level, where there is a hotel and a little museum of seafaring above the rocky beach.

The village of Hartland, inland, is pleasant, but its parish church at nearby Stoke is a real treasure, its size out of all proportion to the local community. Also nearby, you'll find Hartland Abbey, an 18th-century Gothic-style mansion.

ILFRACOMBE MAP REF SS5247

The largest resort on the north Devon coast, Ilfracombe is mostly a Victorian creation, and the fact that it remains popular when so many of Britain's other seaside resorts have gone into a terminal decline is largely due to its setting on one of the most beautiful stretches of coastline in the country. The town is more attractive than many, with some beautiful gardens and a busy little harbour, crammed with pleasure craft and fishing boats.

Ilfracombe is set in a cradle of hills, all with wonderful views – Hillsborough Hill is now a nature reserve, with paths leading up to its 447-foot (136m) summit. Lantern Hill, above the harbour, is surmounted by an ancient chapel, which served as a lighthouse for more than five centuries and is appropriately dedicated to the patron saint of sailors, St Nicholas; the Torrs Walks rise to 447 feet (136m) in gentle fashion, with lots of seats on the way. Walkers can also zig-zag their way up to the 156-foot (48m) summit of Capstone Hill.

Of course, you can't have a seaside resort without a beach, and Ilfracombe has several to fit the bill: the unique Tunnels Beaches are approached from the bottom of Northfield Road via tunnels cut through the cliffs and surrounded by towering rock faces; others are Wildermouth Beach, Cheyne Beach, Larkstone Beach, Rapparee Cove and Hele Bay.

Ilfracombe's attractions include its superb arts complex, the Landmark, in a distinctive modern building on the seafront, a splendid town museum and the well-restored 16th-century corn mill and pottery at Hele Bay, complete with an overshot waterwheel powering the machinery to produce wholemeal flour. Chambercombe Manor, set in a pretty, sheltered combe on the edge of the town, is one of the oldest manor houses in England, dating back to Norman times. Subsequently enlarged, it now has a rambling appearance, an uneven roofline and a cobbled courtyard.

INSTOW MAP REF SS4730

More low-key than most of its famous neighbours, Instow is a charming little place at the wide estuary of the rivers Taw and Torridge, with a sandy beach backed by low dunes. Standing high on a hill overlooking the estuary is Tapeley Park, the home of the Christie family, who are famous for their operatic connections (notably at Glyndebourne), and a collection of operatic costumes is on display in the house. The house (tours by arrangement only) also contains some fine pieces of furniture as well as an interesting collection of porcelain, but the gardens are the real attraction. Rare and tender shrubs, including palms, mimosa and hibiscus, thrive among the beautiful terraces of these sheltered slopes, and there is an organic permaculture garden. And, everywhere you go, there are wonderful views over the Torridge estuary and the north Devon coast.

LUNDY MAP REF SS0345

The sight of a distant island will always stir up our instincts for exploration and adventure, and there are few places

BD 50

BE18

along the north Devon coast which don't have a decent view of Lundy. The trip is expensive, but it is money well spent, for Lundy has an enormous variety of things to see and do. It is reached by boat, the MS *Oldenburg*, from either Bideford or Ilfracombe, and the trip takes two hours. There is also a year-round helicopter service available. Obviously, a clear day is essential if you are not to miss the breathtaking scenery around Lundy's coastline, and do try to avoid excessively windy days, because although Lundy has a generally equable climate, the Atlantic winds sweep uninterrupted across the island from the west.

Just over 3 miles (4.8km) long and about half a mile (800m) across at its widest point, Lundy has granite cliffs rising to over 400 feet (122m) and the land varies from rough grazing in the north to fertile farm land in the south. Although once famous for its successful breeding colony of puffins, numbers fell significantly. Thankfully, after a gap of several years and conservation work by the RSPB, puffins bred again on Lundy in 2005. Visitors will see many other kinds of birds, as well as seals, basking sharks, sika deer, Soay sheep, mountain goats and Lundy ponies. But wildlife is not the only attraction here: there is a great deal of evidence of the island's fascinating history, including an ancient burial chamber and a cave that was used for a while as a prison. You can also see the cannons which were fired in Georgian times as a fog warning and a chasm that opened up when tremors from the Lisbon earthquake in 1755 reached Lundy. The real hub of this little

island's social life is the Marisco Tavern, a friendly pub serving Lundy beer.

All of Lundy is beautiful, but the most spectacular views can be enjoyed from the west side. If wild plants are your particular interest, explore the eastern side, and if you are a climber there are more than 60 challenging rock faces which can be tackled, though many of these are closed during the seabird breeding season (April to July).

LYNTON & LYNMOUTH
MAP REF SS7249

These twin villages are set in some of the best scenery on the north coast. Lynton is perched on top of the 500-foot (152m) cliff, while Lynmouth nestles at its base, where the meandering East Lyn River flows down to meet the sea at the charming little harbour. Pretty cottages line the road beside the river, with a cluster of gift and tea shops, bed and breakfast places and a thatched pub, but although the village has inevitably become somewhat touristy, this does not detract from its undeniable charm.

Lynton is not nearly as picturesque as it neighbour, but it is nevertheless a pleasant little town, and it does have magnificent views along the coast. Among its most interesting buildings is the impressive town hall, just one of the benefits endowed by Sir George Newnes, publisher of the many Sherlock Holmes stories, among other things, who was a frequent visitor here in the 19th century. He also put most of the money into the development of the cliff railway, which links the two communities. Opened at Easter 1890, the railway descends the

500-foot (152m) cliff at a gradient of 1-in-1.75 and its two cars (one going up and one going down) are linked by a steel cable. The descending car is propelled by the weight of 700 gallons (3,182 litres) of water, pumped into its tank at the top of the cliff and emptied at the bottom, and this action hauls the ascending car up to the top.

One of the oldest cottages in Lynton, a delightful 18th-century whitewashed cottage opposite the school, is now the home of the fascinating Lyn and Exmoor Museum, with a collection of bygones that illustrate the life and work of the population. Among its collections are traditional arts and crafts, a scale model of the old Lynton to Barnstaple railway, a reconstruction of an Exmoor kitchen of the 1800s and a section devoted to the tragic Lynmouth flood of 15 August 1952, which claimed 34 lives and devastated the harbour village. It has been estimated that an incredible 90 million gallons (410 million litres) of rain fell in one night on the 40 square miles (103sq km) around Lynmouth. Tiny streams became raging torrents, which combined to pour down the valley, sweeping away the buildings of Lynmouth in their path. The level that the waters attained is marked on a wall at the foot of the Glen Lyn Gorge.

The remarkable Valley of Rocks, 1 mile (1.6km) outside Lynton, is unlike the many combes that go down to the sea along this stretch of coast in that it runs parallel to the coast, a dry valley that was probably formed during the ice ages. The great jagged rocks which protrude skywards from the grassy valley create strange formations, which have been endowed with such fanciful names as the Devil's Cheesewring, Ragged Jack and Castle Rocks. A quite remarkable sight on their own, these rocks are often joined in picturesque pose by one of the wild goats which inhabit the area.

■ **Insight**

PUFFIN ISLAND

The name Lundy is derived from the Norse words *lund*, puffin, and *ey*, island, so we know that the Viking raiders of the 9th century were familiar with this great rock in the Bristol Channel. Perhaps less surprising, is the fact that the island was a haunt of smugglers in the 18th century – they stored their booty in Benson's Cove, in the southeast.

■ **Insight**

A REMARKABLE RESCUE

In 1899, on a stormy night in January, a ship in difficulty was sighted some way along the coast, but because of the high seas and weather conditions, the Lynmouth lifeboat could not be launched. Rather than leave the stricken crew to their fate, a decision was taken to try to haul the lifeboat along the coast to another launching place, a distance of 13 miles (20.8km) which included Countisbury and Porlock Hills. A dozen horses and up to 100 helpers struggled against tremendous odds, widening the road as they went, removing gates and walls, repairing broken wheels on the enormous carriage. At 6 o'clock the following morning the lifeboat was launched and the vessel and its crew were all saved.

SAUNTON SANDS & BRAUNTON BURROWS

MAP REF SS4535

Saunton Sands is one of the best beaches in Devon, a 3-mile (4.8km) curve of golden sands backed by grassy dunes. Towards the northern end of the beach is a car park with a small shop, toilets and a beach bar/café. It is at this end that most visitors congregate, particularly those with young families. Surfers, too, make a beeline from the car park to the sea, but if you walk a little southwards, you will probably find your own sheltered spot among the dunes, complete with an uninterrupted walk across the sands to the sea. Be warned, though, that the very southern end of the beach has treacherous currents which make swimming dangerous.

It is better to turn inland here and explore the Braunton Burrows. This incorporates one of the largest sand dune systems in Britain and is famous for its plant and animal life, receiving Biosphere status from UNESCO in 2002. Marram grass holds the sands in place, and where the ground has stabilised, other plants, such as stonecrop, viper's bugloss and evening primrose, carpet the ground with splashes of colour. In the damper areas there are the marsh varieties of marigolds, orchids and helleborines. Flocks of wading birds populate the estuary, and migrating birds rest here. There is also a huge variety of moths and butterflies. The Ministry of Defence leases an area of the reserve for training, so watch out for the red warning flags, flown when exercises are in progress.

WATERSMEET MAP REF SS7448

This renowned beauty spot, now in the care of the National Trust, can be reached on footpaths along the leafy valley from Lynmouth or by car. Once at Watersmeet, the network of riverside paths expands to give walkers plenty of choice. The waters that meet here are the East Lyn River and Hoaroak Water, both of which take the form of a series of pools, with water tumbling from one to another over the rocks. Lucky visitors may even see salmon leaping in the falls and rapids. The steep sides of the valley are heavily wooded, mostly sessile oak, with some beech and larch, with an undergrowth of ferns, mosses and an abundance of wild flowers. The National Trust has an information centre, shop and tea rooms at Watersmeet House, a former 19th-century fishing lodge.

WOOLACOMBE & MORTEHOE MAP REF SS4643

The lovely sandy beach of Woolacombe and the delightful rocky cove at nearby Mortehoe have made these twin villages a magnet for holidaymakers in the summer, but the surrounding area is still agricultural. Mortehoe sits high on the cliffs above the rocky coastline between Morte Point and Woolacombe sands and has wonderful views and spectacular walks along the Coast Path. Its 12th-century church is said to contain the tomb of one of the murderers of Thomas Becket. Woolacombe is a family resort, with children's entertainment and play areas, and evening activities are mainly of the night club or live pub music variety.

Exmoor and the North Coast's Wooded Combes

This tour takes in the beautiful wooded valleys of the coast, the rolling pastures of its hinterland and the wild open moorland of western Exmoor, before visiting the beauty spot of Watersmeet. The early part of the drive is on steep, narrow roads with hairpin bends. It is slow going and you'll need to take care, but the scenery is well worth the time it takes.

Route Directions

1 Set out with Lynton town hall and tourist information office on your right, and follow signs for the Valley of Rocks, which you will reach shortly after leaving the town.

This beautiful dry valley has huge, fascinating sandstone rock formations created by freeze-thaw action during the ice age, and is populated by wild goats. From the road there are glimpses of the sea and a walk here will be even more rewarding. There is a picnic area on the left at the start of the valley and a large parking area, the last until the end of the valley, on the right.

2 The road passes into the pretty Lee Valley Estate and continues past Lee Abbey Christian Community, where a small toll is payable. Follow the narrow road downhill, then uphill as it turns away from the coast, winding its way through steep, wooded combes, for 0.75 mile (1.2km). At the next junction keep straight ahead, signposted 'Woody Bay'. Pass the Woody

Bay Hotel and later a National Trust car park on the left, then in a mile (1.6km) at a T-junction turn right. In another mile (1.6km) – having passed through Martinhoe, and just past a telephone box – take the right fork downhill, signed 'Hunter's Inn, Heddons Mouth, Trentishoe'. Turn left at Hunter's Inn up a narrow lane. In 2.25 miles (3.6km) meet the A39 and turn right, signposted 'Barnstaple'. After 3.25 miles (5.3km) turn left on to the A399 at Blackmoor Gate, signposted 'South Molton'. Turn right instead at Blackmoor Gate if you want to visit Arlington Court: turn right, then left, signed 'Barnstaple', and continue for 3.25 miles (5.3km) before turning right, signposted 'Arlington Court'.

This charming house (National Trust) dates from 1822 and contains some fascinating collections.

3 On the main route, continue with hilly agricultural land on both sides of the road. In

another 2.25 miles (3.6km) detour right to visit the lovely Exmoor Zoological Park.

The zoo specialises in small exotic animals. You can see wolves, Arctic foxes, lemurs, gibbons and even cheetah.

4 Return to the A399, turn right. In 10 miles (16.1km) at a roundabout, take the 2nd exit, signposted 'South Molton' and continue for 1.5 miles (2.4km) into the town.

South Molton, where you can see some particularly elegant Georgian buildings dotted along the main street, still enjoys a position very much at the heart of the surrounding farming community.

5 From the main street in South Molton, pass the market hall and museum and the health centre on the right and turn left into Station Road, signposted 'North Molton', with lovely views as you leave the town. In just under a mile (1.6km), meet the A361 and turn right, then immediately left, still signposted 'North Molton', and continue for 2.25 miles (3.6km) into the village. Just as you pass a petrol station on the left, turn left, following the signs for 'Heasley Mill' and 'Simonsbath', turning left again at the square. After travelling for 1 mile (1.6km) bear left, signposted 'North Heasley' and 'Simonsbath'. In half a mile (800m) at a crossroads continue forward, signposted 'Simonsbath' and then after 1.75 miles (2.8km) turn right at a T-junction, signposted 'Simonsbath' and 'Exford' to climb steadily on to Exmoor. In 5.25 miles (8.4km) turn left on to the B3223, signposted 'Lynton'. In 6 miles (9.7km) turn right onto the A39, which is signposted 'Lynmouth and Watersmeet'. Watersmeet is one of the county's premier beauty spots. The confluence of the East Lyn River and Hoaroak Water and set in a beautiful, deep, wooded valley, with a wonderful network of footpaths, it also has a National Trust tea room.

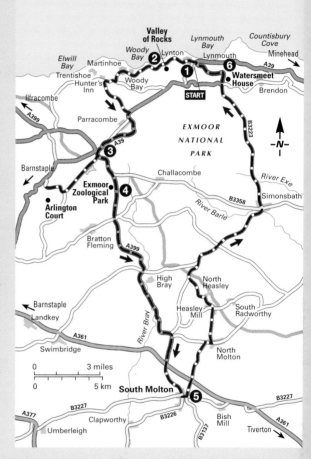

6 Continue down the wooded valley to return to Lynmouth, attractively set around the pretty river valley and tiny harbour, and Lynton, looking out from the cliff top. The two towns are linked by the famous cliff railway.

■ TOURIST INFORMATION CENTRES

Barnstaple
North Devon Museum,
The Square.
Tel: 01271 375000;
www.staynorthdevon.co.uk

Bideford
Victoria Park, The Quay.
Tel: 01237 477676

Braunton
The Bakehouse Centre,
Caen Street.
Tel: 01271 816400;
www.brauntontic.co.uk

Ilfracombe
The Landmark, Sea Front.
Tel: 01271 863001;
www.visitilfracombe.co.uk

Lynton & Lynmouth
Town Hall, Lee Road, Lynton.
Tel: 0845 603232;
www.lynton-lynmouth-
tourism.co.uk

Porlock, West End
Tel: 01643 863150;
www.porlock.co.uk

Woolacombe
The Esplanade.
Tel: 01271 870553; www.
woolacombetourism.co.uk

**Exmoor National Park
Authority (ENPA)
Information Centres**
Cross Street, Combe Martin.
Tel: 01271 883319
www.visitcombemartin.com
Fore Street, Dulverton.
Tel: 01398 323841
Dunster Steep, Dunster.
Tel: 01643 821835

ENPA
Exmoor House, Dulverton.
Tel: 01398 323665; www.
exmoor-nationalpark.gov.uk

■ PLACES OF INTEREST

Arlington Court
Arlington. Tel: 01271 850296;
www.nationaltrust.org.uk

Barnstaple Heritage Centre
Queen Anne's Walk, The
Strand. Tel: 01271 373003

Braunton District Museum
The Bakehouse Centre, Caen
Street. Tel: 01271 816688;
www.devonmuseums.net

Burton Art Gallery & Museum
Wisteria Park, Bideford.
Tel: 01237 471455;
www.burtonartgallery.co.uk

Chambercombe Manor
Ilfracombe.
Tel: 01271 862624; www.
chambercombemanor.org.uk

Clovelly
Tel: 01237 431781;
www.clovelly.co.uk

**Combe Martin Wildlife and
Dinosaur Park**
Tel: 01271 882486;
www.dinosaur-park.com

Dovery Manor Museum
Porlock. Tel: 01643 862420

Dunster Castle
Tel: 01643 821314;
www.nationaltrust.org.uk

Dunster Watermill
Dunster. Tel: 01643 821759;
www.dunsterwatermill.co.uk

Exmoor Pony Centre
Ashwick, Dulverton.

Tel: 01398 323093; www.
moorlandmousietrust.org.uk

Exmoor Zoo
South Stowford, Bratton
Fleming. Tel: 01598 763352;
www.exmoorzoo.co.uk

Hartland Abbey and Gardens
Hartland. Tel: 01237 441264;
www.hartlandabbey.com

Hartland Quay Museum
Hartland. Tel: 01288 331353

Holsworthy Museum
Tel: 01409 259377;
www.devonmuseums.net

Ilfracombe Museum
Wilder Road.
Tel: 01271 863541;
www.devonmuseums.net

Marwood Hill Gardens
Barnstaple.
Tel: 01271 342528; www.
marwoodhillgarden.co.uk

Mortehoe Heritage Centre
Tel: 01271 870028;
www.devonmuseums.net

**Museum of Barnstaple
and North Devon**
The Square, Barnstaple.
Tel: 01271 346747;
www.devonmuseums.net

**North Devon Maritime
Museum**
Odun Road, Appledore.
Tel: 01237 422064;
www.devonmuseums.net

Tapeley Park Gardens
Instow. Tel: 01271 342558

**West Somerset Rural
Life Museum**
The Old School, Allerford.
Tel: 01643 862529

FOR CHILDREN

Devon Badger Watch
Tel: 01398 351506; www.
devonbadgerwatch.co.uk

**Exmoor Owl and
Hawk Centre**
Allerford, nr Porlock.
Tel: 01643 862816; www.
exmoorfalconry.co.uk

Ilfracombe Aquarium
The Old Lifeboat House, The
Pier. Tel: 01271 864533; www.
ilfracombeaquarium.co.uk

Lynton & Barnstaple Railway
Woody Bay Station,
near Parracombe.
Tel: 01598 763487;
www.lynton-rail.co.uk

SHOPPING

Barnstaple
Pannier Market, Tue, Fri, Sat.
Farmers' market, Fri.

Bideford
Pannier Market, Tue and Sat.
Farmers' market, 2nd and
4th Sat.

Combe Martin
Farmers' market, 3rd Sat.

Dulverton
Fortnightly market, Fri.

Ilfracombe
Farmers' market, 3rd Sun.

Lynton
Farmers' market, 1st Sat.

SPORTS, ACTIVITIES

ANGLING

Sea
Appledore. Contact Quay
Cabin. Tel: 01237 477505

Inland
Fishing permits:
South West Lakes Trust.
Tel: 01398 371460;
www.swlakestrust.org.uk

BEACHES

Combe Martin
Pebbles and sand. Dogs are
allowed on the beach.

Croyde
Sand. Dogs restricted.
Lifeguards patrol Easter to
Oct half-term.

Ilfracombe
Tunnels Beaches: shale, grey
sand. Blue Flag; Hele Bay:
shale; Wildermouth: pebble.

Instow
Sand. Dogs restricted.

Putsborough
Sand, rock pools. Dogs
restricted Easter–Oct.

Saunton Sands
Sand. Dogs allowed.

Welcombe
Rocks, sand at low tide;
limited parking.

Westward Ho!
Sand, pebbles. Blue Flag.
Dogs restricted May–Sep.
Lifeguards patrol May–Sep.

Woolacombe
Sand. Blue Flag. Dogs
restricted. Lifeguards patrol
Easter to Oct half-term.

BOAT TRIPS

Appledore
Tarka Cruises; trips from
The Quay. Tel: 01237 476191

Ilfracombe
Paddle steamer *Waverley*

sails from Ilfracombe Pier.
Tel: 0845 1304647; www.
waverleyexcursions.co.uk

**COUNTRY PARKS,
& NATURE RESERVES**
The Cairn and Old Railway,
Ilfracombe.
www.northdevon.gov.uk
Northam Burrows Country
Park. Tel: 01237 479708;
www.torridge.gov.uk
Dunster Forest; Gallox Hill,
near Dunster; Watersmeet.
Tel: 01398 323665. All: www.
exmoor-nationalpark.gov.uk

CYCLE HIRE

Barnstaple
Biketrail, Fremington Quay.
Tel: 01271 372586;
www.biketrail.co.uk
Tarka Trail Cycle Hire,
Railway Station. Tel: 01271
324202; www.tarkabikes.co.uk

Bideford
Bideford Cycle Hire, East-the-
Water. Tel: 01237 424123;
www.bidefordcyclehire.co.uk

HORSE-RIDING

Lynton
Brendon Manor Riding
Stables. Tel: 01598 741246

Woolacombe
Woolacombe Riding Stables,
Eastacott Farm. Tel: 01271
870260; www.woolacombe
ridingstables.co.uk

SAILING

Ilfracombe
Ilfracombe Yacht Club, The
Quay. Tel: 01271 863969;
www.ilfracombeyc.org.uk

Tea Rooms

Lewis's Tea Rooms
13 High Street, Dulverton
TA22 9HB
Tel: 01398 323850

This is a really traditional tea shop, complete with pretty little courtyard and flowery tablecloths. Try the light lunches (excellent rarebit), traditional home-made cakes and excellent cream teas.

Kitnor's Tea Room
Bossington TA24 8HQ
Tel: 01643 862643

If you're after tea in a lovely 15th-century cottage and garden, Kitnor's is the place to go. It's tucked away in Bossington, just a mile (1.6km) inland from Porlock Bay. Scones and cakes (including apple, carrot and walnut, and lemon drizzle) are all home-made and there are gluten-free options.

Quay Café
Fremington Quay,
Bickington, nr Barnstaple
EX31 2NH
Tel: 01271 378783; www.
fremingtonquaycafe.co.uk

This award-winning café is in a renovated railway station on the Tarka Trail overlooking the Taw estuary. Dishes use fresh local vegetables, fish, game and West Country wine, beer and cider. Try the delicious cream tea.

Docton Mill Gardens
Lymebridge, Hartland
EX39 6EA
Tel: 01237 441369
www.doctonmill.co.uk

Enjoy a slice of cake in the tranquil surroundings of this beautiful woodland and wildflower garden in Spekes valley. There has been a mill here since Domesday; the buildings, wheel, leats and ponds have been beautifully restored. Strawberries, raspberries and salads are all grown in the garden.

Pubs

The Royal Oak Inn
Withypool TA24 7QP
Tel: 01643 831506; www.
royaloakwithypool.co.uk

Subtle lighting, open fires, dark wooden tables, low beams and various hunting memorabilia create the atmosphere here. Ingredients are sourced locally when possible, such as partridge and venison, Quicke's farmhouse cheddar and Somerset brie.

The Royal Oak Inn
Luxborough TA23 0SH
Tel: 01984 640319; www.
theroyaloakinnluxborough.
co.uk

This low-beamed, traditional, unspoiled country inn, with inglenook fireplaces and flagstone floors, has a reputation for excellent food. Try roast rack of lamb, basil, garlic and pine nut risotto, or filo parcel of smoked haddock, spinach and Devon Oke (local cheddar).

The Royal George
Appledore EX39 1RJ
Tel: 01237 474335

The beamed, 18th-century Royal George has superb views across the Taw estuary. Photos on the walls recall Appledore's shipbuilding heyday. Try a main course of fresh local fish followed by Hocking's ice cream or bread-and-butter pudding.

The Old Smithy Inn
Welcombe, Bideford
EX39 6HG
Tel: 01288 331305;
www.oldsmithyinn.co.uk

A couple of miles north of the Cornish border, this wonderful black-and-white thatched pub dates from the 16th century. It's comfortable and friendly, with slate floors, archive photographs, a huge fireplace and even a piano. Food is sourced locally, and fish and seafood are popular, but if you don't fancy fish, you could try the chorizo and beef burger or roast vegetable and Cornish blue cheese tart.

CADBURY CASTLE

Devon's Rural Heartland

INTRODUCTION

Major tourist attractions are few and far between in this area, which, in a way, makes it all the more interesting to visit because here you will find the real heart and the real people of Devon. Its towns are generally unspoiled by modern development and remain centres for the surrounding agricultural areas, with 'proper' markets and practical shops, and if you delve beneath their workaday life, you will find a fascinating history. Outside the towns, amongst the patchwork of fields and alarmingly narrow lanes, are some of Devon's prettiest villages, such as Sheepwash and Winkleigh.

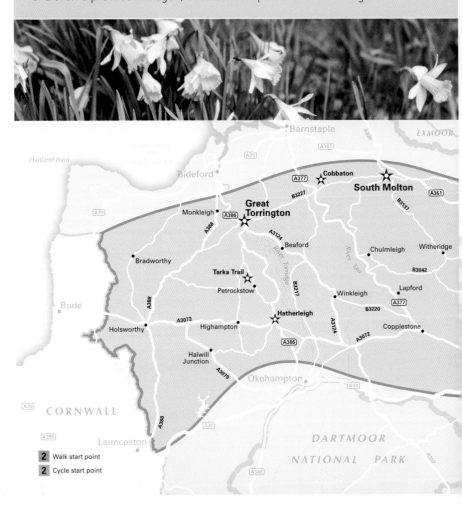

☆ **2** Walk start point

☆ **2** Cycle start point

SHEEPWASH

NATIONAL PARK

SOMERSET

Bampton

Wellington

Tiverton
Sampford Peverell

Bickleigh

Crediton

Honiton

Exeter

Exmouth

TARKA TRAIL

Unmissable attractions

With fewer obvious things to go and see, the heart of Devon is a region where you feel almost obliged to slow down and enjoy a more relaxed pace of life, with the pretty countryside hiding delightful towns such as Great Torrington, South Molton and Hatherleigh. In terms of outdoor activities, this part of Devon is perfect for those with a spirit of adventure. The terrain lends itself well to horse riding and cycling – while a section of the 180-mile (290km) Tarka Trail, which offers safe cycling on a clearly signposted route, runs through the area. It's not all wild landscape though, and the lavish Victorian country house Knightshayes Court, which is managed by the National Trust, has beautiful gardens with many rare plants and woodland walks.

1 Bickleigh
An incredibly beautiful and timeless scene captured as the River Exe flows through the quiet village of Bickleigh.

2 The Tarka Trail
Get on your bike and cycle part of the clearly signed 180-mile (290km) Tarka Trail.

3 Hatherleigh
Pretty Hatherleigh is worth a wander for its antique shops and weekly livestock market, which draws farmers from all over the region.

4 Grand Western Canal, Tiverton
A canal longboat carrying day-trippers is towed along the bank of the Grand Western Canal at Tiverton by a draught horse. The canal runs between Tiverton and Taunton and you can get on the water yourself by hiring a rowing boat, or cycle along the tow path.

BICKLEIGH MAP REF SS9407

Bickleigh is a pretty village of thatched cottages on either side of the River Exe, linked by a narrow 300-year-old bridge that was reputedly the inspiration for Paul Simon's song *Bridge over Troubled Water*. Close by the bridge is Bickleigh Mill, a watermill which has been converted into a craft centre.

Standing just outside the village, off the Crediton road, is Bickleigh Castle, a fortified manor house with a fascinating history. The fortunes of the castle and its various occupants have been mixed, to say the least. In the early 16th century it came into the ownership of the Carew family, after the runaway marriage of Elizabeth Courtenay, the granddaughter of the Earl of Devon, and Thomas Carew, the younger brother of her guardian. Sadly, as a result of the family's Royalist sympathies during the Civil War, a large part of Bickleigh Castle was demolished. Fortunately, some of its many buildings, including the gatehouse, were restored at the beginning of the 20th century and form a delightful complex that bears witness to the many centuries that have passed since the castle was first built. Unfortunately the castle is now only available for weddings and is no longer open to the public. Bickleigh is at the mid-point of the Exe Valley Way, a long-distance route which follows this lovely valley from Exford on Exmoor to Starcross on the Exe estuary.

A little further from Bickleigh, also off the Crediton road, is Fursdon House. This has been the home of one of Devon's oldest families since the 13th century, though the present house is a mere 400 years old! It contains historic costumes, mementoes and archives as well as portraits.

COBBATON MAP REF SS6126

Within a maze of lanes to the southeast of Barnstaple is, perhaps, one of the most surprising attractions in the whole county, the Cobbaton Combat Collection. Crammed into two large exhibition halls is a vast collection of military vehicles, guns, weapons and other equipment from all over the world. You can walk among them and peer into them; some are arranged as tableaux, depicting how they would have been used. This private collection is the result of the obsession of one man, Preston Isaac, who began amassing militaria some 50 years ago. There are exhibits from the Second World War and the Warsaw Pact countries, as well as reference displays on the First World War, the Falklands conflict and the first Gulf War. One of the more recent acquisitions is a Chieftain tank from the armed crossing point, Checkpoint Charlie, in Berlin.

Reconstructions of civilian wartime scenes feature in the considered Home Front displays and the exhibition halls resound with the sounds of Glen Miller, the Andrews Sisters as well as formal recorded news items. The theme of this fascinating collection never wavers – the children's play area has a Sherman tank to clamber over and refreshments are served from a NAAFI wagon.

CREDITON MAP REF SS8300

This is a pleasant and attractive town and though many of its historically important buildings have gone, destroyed by a series of fires over the years, there remains an air of former glory about the place. This becomes most apparent when the parish church comes into view – a huge and impressive building of cathedral proportions. The fact is that there was once a cathedral here, indeed Crediton's distinguished history is largely based upon its religious heritage. It all started in AD 680, when a baby boy, christened Winfrith, was born here. He went on to become a great Christian missionary, one of the founding fathers of Europe's Christian Church and the patron saint of Germany and the Netherlands as St Boniface. He is also credited with finding the first Christmas tree: a fir tree growing from the roots of a felled pagan oak.

The first diocesan church was built here in AD 909 and served as a cathedral until 1050, when the bishopric moved to Exeter. The present building has some Norman parts, but mostly dates from around 1410. The collegiate church was so important to the townspeople that when Henry VIII dissolved it in 1547, they negotiated its purchase for £300 and set up a board of twelve governors to control its affairs, a practice that has survived to this day.

Before the mid-19th century there were no shops in Crediton's High Street; instead, everything was bought from stalls along the middle of the road. These markets originated in 1231, and from 1306 until fairly recently a cattle fair was held each spring. It was the largest of its kind in the West Country, with the High Street, then the new cattle market,

■ Insight

KING OF THE GYPSIES

The Carews of Bickleigh Castle fame were certainly not a dull family, but the most notorious of all must be Bampfylde Moore Carew, who was born into an advantaged life but went off the rails in a spectacular way. While Bampfylde was a schoolboy, at the famous Blundell's School in Tiverton, he fell in with a band of gypsies and ran away to lead the life of a Romany. A born leader and accomplished confidence trickster, he eventually became the King of the Gypsies and tales of his exploits have become legendary. Bampfylde is buried in an unmarked grave in the churchyard at Bickleigh.

■ Activity

A SCENIC ROUTE

By far the best approach to Crediton is along the A3072 from Bickleigh. This switchback road passes through some of Devon's loveliest countryside and offers one breathtaking view after another.

■ Insight

ON PARADE

Crediton's Belle Parade gets its name from the period between 1805 and 1812, when French naval prisoners of war, in their smart blue and yellow uniforms, were allowed to parade here.

■ Visit

CREDITON'S HERMIT

One of Crediton's most ancient buildings is the chapel of St Lawrence, found off Threshers Road at the west end of the High Street. Built around 1200, it included a cell for a religious hermit who would dispense counsel to those who came to him for advice. The building has been restored, but the two end walls are original.

Bickleigh and the Exe Valley

Leave the crowds behind at picturesque Bickleigh Bridge and explore the lovely Exe Valley along country lanes and tracks. Bickleigh Castle is approached along a quiet lane, shaded by huge oak, ash and beech trees. Bickleigh Mill, the working watermill at the start of the walk, has craft and gift shops. Near by is the Devon Railway Centre, the largest collection of narrow-gauge exhibits in the Southwest, with train rides and model railways.

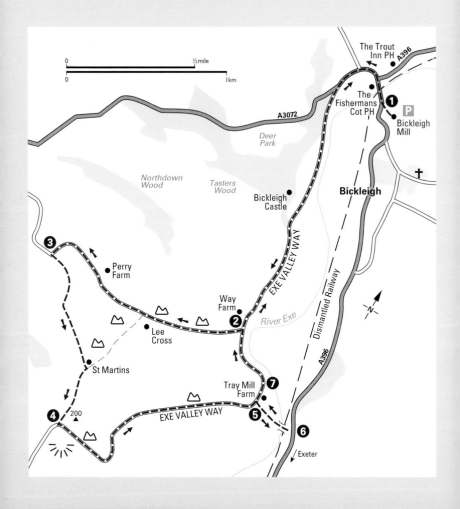

Route Directions

1 From near Bickleigh Mill go back, with care, to the A396 and cross the bridge. Turn left down the A3072, following the brown tourist sign for Bickleigh Castle. Take the first lane left, running along the edge of the flood plain on the Exe Valley Way (EVW). Bickleigh Castle will soon be found on the right. Go straight on along the lane.

2 Pass Way Farm and take the next lane right to leave the Exe Valley Way, roughly signposted 'Lee Cross & Perry Farm'. Take care, this is a very narrow lane, carrying traffic from local farms. Keep along the lane as it climbs steeply uphill and after 700yds (640m) brings you to the farm at Lee Cross. Keep ahead up the lane to pass Perry Lodge. Eventually the lane bears sharp left and then right.

3 Turn left on a green lane and walk uphill, with increasingly good views over the Exe Valley and back to Bickleigh. Pass a restored chapel – St Martins – on the left, and keep ahead; at last the track levels off.

4 Where the green lane meets the tarmac lane turn left and proceed steeply downhill (EVW). The views over the River Exe, and to Silverton church beyond, are glorious. Follow the lane down until you see Tray Mill Farm on the right.

5 The way home is straight on, but it's worth making a short detour to the river. Turn right through the farmyard and pass through a metal gate on to a concrete standing. Cross the field, aiming for the suspension bridge. Cross over (not for the faint-hearted!) to reach the dismantled railway track. Do not turn left along the track – although it would take you back to your car– it is privately owned and has no public right of way.

6 The path goes straight on here to meet the A369. You can do that, turn left, then eventually right to walk through Bickleigh village to the mill, but it is a busy road and you would be better advised to retrace your steps to Tray Mill Farm and take the quieter route back to Bickleigh Mill.

7 Back on the lane by Tray Mill Farm, turn right and walk straight along the lane, past Bickleigh Castle, turning right at the A3072, and right again over the bridge to return to your car.

Route facts

DISTANCE/TIME 5.75 miles (9.2km) 2h15

MAP OS Explorer 114 Exeter and the Exe Valley

START Overflow parking area Bickleigh Mill off the A396; grid ref: SX 938075

TRACKS Country lanes, one long, steep track

GETTING TO THE START Bickleigh Mill off the A396, 4 miles (6.4km) south of Tiverton.

THE PUB The Fisherman's Cot, Bickleigh EX16 8RW. Tel: 01884 855237; www.marstonsinns.co.uk

❶ One long steep track; suspension bridge (can be avoided).

What to look for

Watch the salmon leaping up the weir just below the bridge. On this stretch of the Exe the fishing rights are privately owned. Salmon and sea trout fishing licences are available from the Environment Agency, and the season on the Exe runs from mid-February to the end of September for salmon and from mid-March to end September for sea trout and brown trout. Strict conservation measures protect spring salmon.

GREAT TORRINGTON

MAP REF SS4919

If the approach to Torrington seems rather dull, don't be disheartened because this is a delightful little town with a great deal to see and do.

Turn off the through-road into the town centre and you will discover the heart of the place – a charming square that is most people's idea of what a real town centre should be. There is a lovely old inn, which has Civil War connections, a fine town hall and a market hall, and just around the corner from the square the Plough Arts Centre has a lively programme of jazz, theatre, film and stand-up comedy.

Great Torrington is set high on a hill overlooking lush agricultural land. On three sides it has common land, preserved by an Act of Parliament, and below it flows the wide River Torridge. The Dartington Crystal factory was established in the town in the 1960s, when Swedish craftsmen were brought here to train a local workforce in the art of glass-blowing. The company rapidly expanded, exporting its fine crystal all over the world, but its operation here is very much geared to the large number of visitors it receives. The factory tours are fascinating, and high walkways enable visitors to look down over the teams of craftsmen and witness their glass-blowing skills. Every stage in the production, from furnace to packing case, can be seen, plus there is a very good video introduction and a display of glassware in the entrance hall.

After the tour there is, of course, the opportunity to buy, from a vast showroom. Another showroom sells pottery, gift items and kitchenware, and there is an airy cafeteria.

Just south of the town on the B3220 Exeter road, RHS Garden Rosemoor has long been famous and is continuing to expand and develop new areas of cultivation. The original 8 acres (3.2ha) were created by Lady Anne Barry to surround her home, but in 1988 she gave them, along with a further 32 acres (13ha) of land, to the Royal Horticultural Society, which has wasted no time in making full use of the golden opportunity provided. A National Garden has been thoughtfully created here, and the previously uncultivated land has been planted with a number of gardens. There are two rose gardens containing around 2,000 roses in 200 varieties, wonderful herbaceous borders, a herb garden and potager, colour-themed gardens, an extensive stream and bog garden centred on an ornamental lake, a cottage garden and a foliage garden. Fruit and vegetable cultivation has not been left out either and exciting new developments are always under way.

There is a good visitor centre with a restaurant and shop, as well as plants for sale, many propagated from specimens in the gardens.

HATHERLEIGH MAP REF SS5404

If you approach Hatherleigh from the north you will be entering the charming market town the best way, on a road which twists and turns down a steep hillside lined with pretty colour-washed cottages and ancient pubs, including the lovely Tally Ho Inn. If you approach

Hatherleigh at all on a Tuesday morning, be prepared to do it slowly, because you will probably be behind a string of farmers heading for the market in anything from a large modern cattle truck to an old estate car with a couple of sheep in the back! All local life converges on Hatherleigh on market day. If you spend a couple of hours wandering around the market and the town, you'll find that it beats any organised tourist attraction. The poultry auction is particularly entertaining, and the little cheese shop has a wonderful selection, including local produce. The town itself has antiques and junk shops and its own pottery on the main street.

SOUTH MOLTON   MAP REF SS7125

Once on the main holiday route to the north coast, South Molton, now free of through traffic, is a delightful little town. In spite of the very grand town hall and the many antiques shops, craft and art galleries, it is still a working town, with supermarkets, banks, bakers' shops and the like. By no means 'touristy', South Molton nevertheless has a variety of attractions, including Quince Honey Farm. Established in 1949, this is Britain's largest honey farm, and its work is illustrated with a very good video and with hives full of bees. About 20 different kinds of habitat have been set up behind glass, and the innovative design of the exhibition hives enable visitors to open them at the press of a button to show the bees living and working inside. A wide variety of honey and beeswax products are on sale in an extensive shop area.

Visit

TARKA COUNTRY

Great Torrington overlooks the Torridge and its tributaries – Tarka the Otter country. Numbers have increased in the county over recent years, but visitors are unlikely to see the shy, mostly nocturnal creatures in the wild. If you want to be certain to see some otters, there is an Otter Trust sanctuary over the border in Cornwall, situated at North Petherwin near Launceston (about 25 miles/40km from Barnstaple). Several otter species, including the Eurasian (living wild in this country) can be seen at the Dartmoor Otter Sanctuary at Buckfastleigh. Otters are also on view at Combe Martin Wildlife and Dinosaur Park.

Activity

MID-TORRIDGE CYCLE LINK

This attractive route links the famous Tarka Trail cycle/walkway at Petrockstowe with the Sticklepath cycle route as it passes through Hatherleigh on its way to Dartmoor. These three cycle trails, when combined, form a continuous route from Dartmoor to the north Devon coast.

Visit

TEAMWORK

The organised, almost choreographed, way in which the glass-blowers at the Dartington Crystal factory interact makes compulsive viewing. Without a word or a glance, they cross and recross each other's paths as they move backwards and forwards from furnace to workplace, passing the hot glass for each stage of the process, in what appears to the uninitiated to be a series of near-misses.

TARKA TRAIL

Most people know of Tarka the Otter, the subject of that wonderful book (and later film) by Henry Williamson, and it was during his sojourn here in the 1920s that Williamson found his inspiration when he became the adoptive 'parent' of an orphaned otter cub.

These days Tarka is everywhere, giving his name not only to tea shops and guesthouses but also a long-distance trail through the countryside, which his creator wrote about. The trail is based as far as possible on the route taken by Tarka along the rivers Taw and Torridge and extends for an incredible 180 miles (290km) from Dartmoor to Exmoor and the north coast, with access points along the way. Over 30 miles (48km) are on the trackbeds of disused railway lines and these are designated cycleways. The section between Barnstaple and Great Torrington forms the Tarka Country Park, and horse-riding is allowed between Torrington and Petrockstowe.

■ Insight

GRAND WESTERN CANAL

The system of canals known as the Grand Western was originally intended to link the Bristol Channel and the English Channel, but for financial reasons the scheme never reached completion – the parts from Taunton to Burlescombe and the branch to Tiverton are all that were built. After the railway came to Tiverton in the 1840s, the canal declined, but it was rescued and restored during the 1960s, becoming a country park where the wildlife and the tranquil surroundings can be enjoyed. Horse-drawn boat trips are also available from the canal basin in Tiverton.

TIVERTON MAP REF SS9512

For a town to prosper these days, its proximity to the motorway network is of considerable importance; in the old days it was the rivers that provided the lifeline. Tiverton, with its two rivers, the Grand Western Canal and the M5 just a short distance away, has always been advantaged and it remains a lively centre. Tiverton's appearance owes much to the prosperity of its textile and clothing industries in the 16th and 17th centuries, when rich wool merchants endowed their town with such splendid buildings as St Peter's Church, Blundell's School, the Great House and three sets of almshouses. St George's Church, built in 1773, is said to be one of the finest Georgian churches in Devon.

Tiverton's history is documented in the town museum, in St Andrew Street. It includes the Heathcoat Lace Gallery, an agricultural section, two waterwheels and a railway gallery.

Tiverton's two rivers are the Exe and the Lowman (Tiverton means 'two-ford town'), and the former is overlooked by Tiverton Castle. Dating from 1106, all that remains of the original building is one circular tower.

North of Tiverton is Knightshayes Court (National Trust). This ornate 19th-century mansion was built for Sir John Heathcoat-Amory. Designed by William Burges, it features rich Gothic-style decoration, painted ceilings and wall stencilling. The house is more than equally matched by the wonderful grounds that surround it, comprising a pleasing formal gardens, woodland and ornamental shrubs.

Along the Grand Western Canal to Tiverton

This peaceful ride along the banks of the old Grand Western Canal passes through the GWC Country Park and the beautiful countryside of mid-Devon before reaching the centre of Tiverton. The canal provides ideal wildlife habitats – there are coots, moorhens and mallards on the water, and robins, starlings, chaffinches and blackbirds around many picnic spots. You may see herons or kingfishers by the water. It's a wonderful place for wildflowers and butterflies, too.

Route Directions

1 From the back of the car park, pass the tennis court (left), bear left round a gate and uphill to the tow path (don't go too fast or you might easily overshoot!). Construction of the canal began in 1810, part of a scheme to link the English and Bristol Channels via Exeter and Bristol, but only the Tiverton and Taunton stretch was completed, in 1814. Competition from the railways eventually forced the closure of the canal, although this section was still being used to transport limestone from quarries in the area around Westleigh to Tiverton as late as 1924.

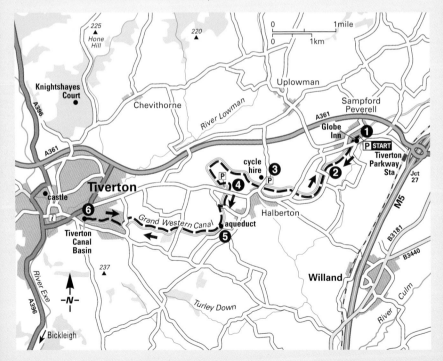

2 Turn left along the tow path, passing The Globe Inn. Pass under Sampford Peverell bridge (best to dismount) and continue along a short stretch of quiet lane. Where that bears left, keep ahead along the canalside and you will find yourself immediately out in the countryside, with good views of the wooded Blackdown Hills to the left – you may well feel as if you're miles away from anywhere. Pass under Battens Bridge, then Rock Bridge. The next bridge is constructed from metal. These – look out for them along the route – were originally wooden swing bridges, which allowed the passage of barges and linked farmers' land where it was split by the canal.

3 Continue cycling along an embanked stretch to pass under the Greenway Bridge (car park) and then Sellake Bridge. Note how the canal takes a wide sweep to the left; this is known as the Swan's Neck, and was necessary to avoid the village of Halberton.

4 Next stop is Tiverton Road Bridge (car park and picnic area), where you may see canoes and kayaks. There was once a stone-crushing yard here; the journey from a quarry 8 miles (12.9km) away

at Whipcott took 2.5 hours, with two horses pulling three 10-ton barges. Note milestone III on the left; it's only 3 miles (4.8km) further to the basin at Tiverton. Keep on to Crownhill Bridge, once known as Change Path. Horses had to change to the right bank here; you do the same by crossing the bridge and turning left.

5 Cross the brick aqueduct of the Bristol and Exeter Railway line, built in 1847. This – the Tiverton branch – closed to passenger traffic in 1964. Three more bridges bring you to neat hedges and bungalows marking the edge of Tiverton. Tidcombe Bridge (look out for milestone I) marks another loop, made necessary by the Bishop of Exeter's refusal to allow the canal within 100yds (91m) of his home, grand Tidcombe Hall, which is nearby.

6 Built in 1842, Tiverton Canal Basin makes an excellent focus for this ride. You can buy refreshments en route at the thatched 16th-century Canal Tearooms, below the basin, or from the Duck's Ditty Floating Café Bar. Look out too for the old lime kilns to the right. Until the late 19th century limestone was burnt here to produce fertiliser. Farmers are said to

have travelled up to 30 miles (48km) each way by horse and cart to collect it. To return to the start point at Sampford Peverell, simply retrace your steps back along the canal tow path to the car park.

Route facts

DISTANCE/TIME 11 miles (17.6km) 2h15

MAP OS Explorer 128 Taunton & Blackdown Hills and 114 Exeter & the Exe Valley

START Sampford Peverell, grid ref: ST 030142

TRACKS Good canalside path, some stretches grassy, most gritty

GETTING TO THE START Sampford Peverell lies west of M5 junction 27 (Tiverton Parkway). From the M5 follow the A361 Tiverton road; at the first exit (0.5 mile/800m) leave the A361, bear left at the roundabout and continue into the village. The public car park is signed to the right.

CYCLE HIRE Abbotshood Cycle Hire, Halberton. Tel: 01884 820728; www.abbotshoodcyclehire.co.uk

THE PUB The Globe Inn, Sampford Peverell. Tel: 01884 821214; www.globe-inn.com

❶ Path narrow under bridges – cyclists are advised to dismount.

■ TOURIST INFORMATION CENTRES

Great Torrington
Castle Hill. Tel: 01805 626140;
www.great-torrington.com

Holsworthy
The Square.
Tel: 01409 254185;
www.holsworthy.co.uk

South Molton
East Street.
Tel: 01769 574122;
www.visitsouthmolton.co.uk

Tiverton
Phoenix Lane.
Tel: 01884 255827;
www.discovertiverton.co.uk

■ PLACES OF INTEREST

Bickleigh Castle
Tel: 01884 855363;
www.bickleighcastle.com
Group bookings only.

Cobbaton Combat Collection
Cobbaton, Chittlehampton.
Tel: 01769 540740;
www.cobbatoncombat.co.uk

Dartington Crystal
Great Torrington.
Tel: 01805 626262;
www.dartington.co.uk

Fursdon House
Cadbury, Thorverton.
Tel: 01392 860860;
www.fursdon.co.uk

Knightshayes Court
Bolham, nr Tiverton.
Tel: 01884 254665;
www.nationaltrust.org.uk

Quince Honey Farm
South Molton.

Tel: 01769 572401;
www.quincehoney.co.uk

RHS Garden Rosemoor
Great Torrington.
Tel: 01805 626810;
www.rhs.org.uk

South Molton & District Museum
The Square.
Tel: 01769 572951; www.
southmoultonmuseum.org

Tiverton Castle
Tiverton. Tel: 01884 253200;
www.tivertoncastle.com

Tiverton Museum
Beck's Square.
Tel: 01884 256295;
www.tivertonmuseum.org.uk

Torrington Museum and Archive
High Street.
Tel: 01805 624324;
www.great-torrington.com

■ FOR CHILDREN

Devon Badger Watch
North of Tiverton.
Tel: 01398 351506;
www.devonbadgerwatch.co.uk

Devon Railway Centre
Bickleigh, nr Tiverton.
Tel: 01884 855671; www.
devonrailwaycentre.co.uk

North Devon Farm Park
Marsh Farm, Landkey.
Tel: 01271 830255;
www.devonfarmpark.co.uk

Quad World
Langford, nr Cullompton.
Tel: 01392 881313;
www.quadworld.co.uk

■ SHOPPING

Crediton
Farmers' market, 1st Sat.

Cullompton
Farmers' market, 2nd Sat.

Hatherleigh
Cattle market and Pannier Market, Tue.

Great Torrington
Market, Thu and Sat.

Holsworthy
Pannier Market, Wed;
livestock, Wed and Sat.

South Molton
Farmers' market, 4th Sat.
Pannier Market, Thu,
livestock, Thu.

Tiverton
Pannier market, 3rd Wed.

LOCAL SPECIALITIES

Cider
Gray's Devon Cider
Halstow, Tedburn St Mary.
Tel: 01647 61236
Palmerhayes Devon Cider
& Scrumpy, Calverleigh.
Tel: 01884 254579

Clotted Cream
Many shops provide clotted cream mail order service.

Crafts
Bickleigh Mill
Bickleigh. Tel: 01884 855419;
www.bickleighmill.com

Glass
The Dartington Crystal Visitor Centre, Great Torrington.
Tel: 01805 626262;
www.dartington.co.uk

Honey, Candles and Beeswax
Quince Honey Farm

South Molton.
Tel: 01769 572401;
www.quincehoney.co.uk

Local Food and Crafts
Griffins Yard
South Molton.
Tel: 01769 572372; www.
craftsgallerygriffinsyard.co.uk

Pottery
Barton Pottery
South Barton, Tiverton.
Tel: 01823 672987;
www.bartonpottery.co.uk
Hatherleigh Pottery, 20
Market Street, Hatherleigh.
Tel: 01837 810624;
www.hatherleighpottery.co.uk

Wine
Yearlstone Vineyard
Bickleigh, Tiverton.
Tel: 01884 855700;
www.yearlstone.co.uk

■ PERFORMING ARTS

Crediton Arts Centre
East Street, Crediton.
Tel: 01363 773260;
www.creditonartscentre.org
Plough Arts Centre
Great Torrington.
Tel: 01805 624624;
www.plough-arts.org

■ SPORTS & ACTIVITIES

ANGLING
Fly Fishing
Bellbrook Valley Trout
Fishery, Oakford, Tiverton.
Tel: 01398 351292;
www.bellbrookfishery.co.uk.
Book in advance.

Coarse Fishing
Creedy Lakes, Long Barn,
Crediton. Tel: 01363 772684;
www.creedylakes.com
Grand Western Canal,
Tiverton. Day and season
tickets from tackle shops.
Lower Hollacombe Fishery,
Crediton. Tel: 01363 84331
Oaktree Fishery, South
Molton. Tel: 01398 341568;
www.oaktreefishery.co.uk
Salmon Hutch Coarse
Fishery, Crediton.
Tel: 01363 772749

BOAT TRIPS
The Tiverton Canal Company.
Tel: 01884 253345;
www.tivertoncanal.co.uk

**COUNTRY PARKS, FORESTS
& NATURE RESERVES**
Abbeyford Woods.
www.forestry.gov.uk
Eggesford Forest.
www.forestry.gov.uk
Grand Western Canal Country
Park, Tiverton.
Tel: 01884 254072;
www.devon.gov.uk

CYCLING
For The Tarka Trail and
Mid-Torridge Cycle Link:
www.tarka-country.co.uk

CYCLE HIRE
Grand Western Canal
Abbotshood Cycle Hire.
Tel: 01884 820728; www.
abbotshoodcyclehire.co.uk
Great Torrington
Torridge Cycle Hire, The
Station. Tel: 01805 622633

GOLF COURSES
Chulmleigh
Chulmleigh Golf Course,
Leigh Road.
Tel: 01769 580519;
www.chulmleighgolf.co.uk
Crediton
Downes Crediton Golf Club.
Tel: 01363 773025;
www.downescreditongc.co.uk
Tedburn St Mary
Fingle Glen Hotel Golf
& Country Club Centre.
Tel: 01647 61817; www.
fingleglengolfhotel.co.uk
Tiverton
Tiverton Golf Club, Post Hill.
Tel: 01884 252187;
www.tivertongolfclub.co.uk

HORSE-RIDING
Calverleigh
Rose and Crown Riding
Stables, Palmer's Lodge.
Tel: 01884 252060
Chulmleigh
Bold Try Equestrian Centre,
Leigh Road.
Tel: 01769 580366
Cullompton
Heazle Riding Centre,
Clayhidon. Tel: 01823 680280;
www.heazle.co.uk

■ ANNUAL EVENTS & CUSTOMS

Crediton
Boniface Festival, early Jun.
Hatherleigh
Music Festival, early Jul.
South Molton
Olde English Fayre, mid-Jun.

Tea Rooms

The Corn Dolly
**115a East Street,
South Molton EX36 3DB
Tel: 01769 574249**
Wooden tables, bone china, corn dollies and a tempting display of cakes create a real 'old farmhouse kitchen' feel. Try the Corn Dolly teacake, light cheese scones or the Gamekeeper's Tea, Seafarer's Tea or a Queen's Ransom (crumpets and Stilton), or go for the Corn Dolly cream tea.

Four & Twenty Blackbirds Tea Shoppe
**43 Gold Street, Tiverton
EX16 6QB Tel: 01884 257055**
Low beams, vases of flowers, and antique furniture create a homely atmosphere at this traditional tea shop near the clock tower. Choose from different 'teas': Maid's (apple tart), King's (cheese and chutney), Queen's (egg), Jenny Wren's (scones, jelly, ice cream) and Blackbird's (sandwiches and cake).

Canal Tea Room
**Lime Kiln Cottage, Grand Western Canal, Tiverton
EX16 4AQ
Tel: 01884 252291**
Enjoy home-made cakes, scones and local ice cream at this lovely tea garden attached to a thatched cottage with a pond and covered seating. It's situated just below the basin of the Grand Western Canal.

Crediton Station Tea Rooms
**Crediton EX17 5BY
Tel: 01363 777766**
Thoughts of *Brief Encounter* abound in this wood-panelled platform tea room, which is steeped in railway history. Try Tuckman's Tucker, Porter's Provender or Controller's Nosh!

Pubs

Lamb Inn
**The Square, Sandford, Crediton EX17 4LW
Tel: 01363 773676;
www.lambinnsandford.co.uk**
This is a real village pub (originally a 16th-century post house) where you can slump in a sofa in front of the fire with a paper, play a board game, enjoy real ale or local cider or have a superb meal from the short but interesting menu. Try the excellent West Country cheese board.

The Mountpleasant Inn
**Nomansland, Tiverton
EX16 8NN
Tel: 01884 860271**
A bustling, friendly, family-run pub that welcomes everyone, especially other families. Set in the heart of the county, this popular inn dates from the 18th century, when it began life as a simple ostler's house. Today there is an attractive restaurant in the former blacksmith's forge, which serves a variety of reasonably priced food.

The Duke of York
**Iddesleigh, Winkleigh
EX19 8BG
Tel: 01837 810253**
Look no further if you want an authentic, unpretentious country pub catering mainly for locals, not tourists. Expect oak beams, open fires and antique photos. Meals, which include fish pie and local honey-roast jumbo sausages, are reasonably priced and the portions are generous.

The Beer Engine
**Newton St Cyres EX5 5AX
Tel: 01392 851282;
www.thebeerengine.co.uk**
Excellent food and real ale, are both served in this welcoming pub, originally a railway hotel built around 1850. Choosing what to eat is difficult: Sleeper Ale steak pie, cod in Beer Engine batter plus innovative vegetarian dishes and delicious puds. Board games, newspapers and local information complete the experience.

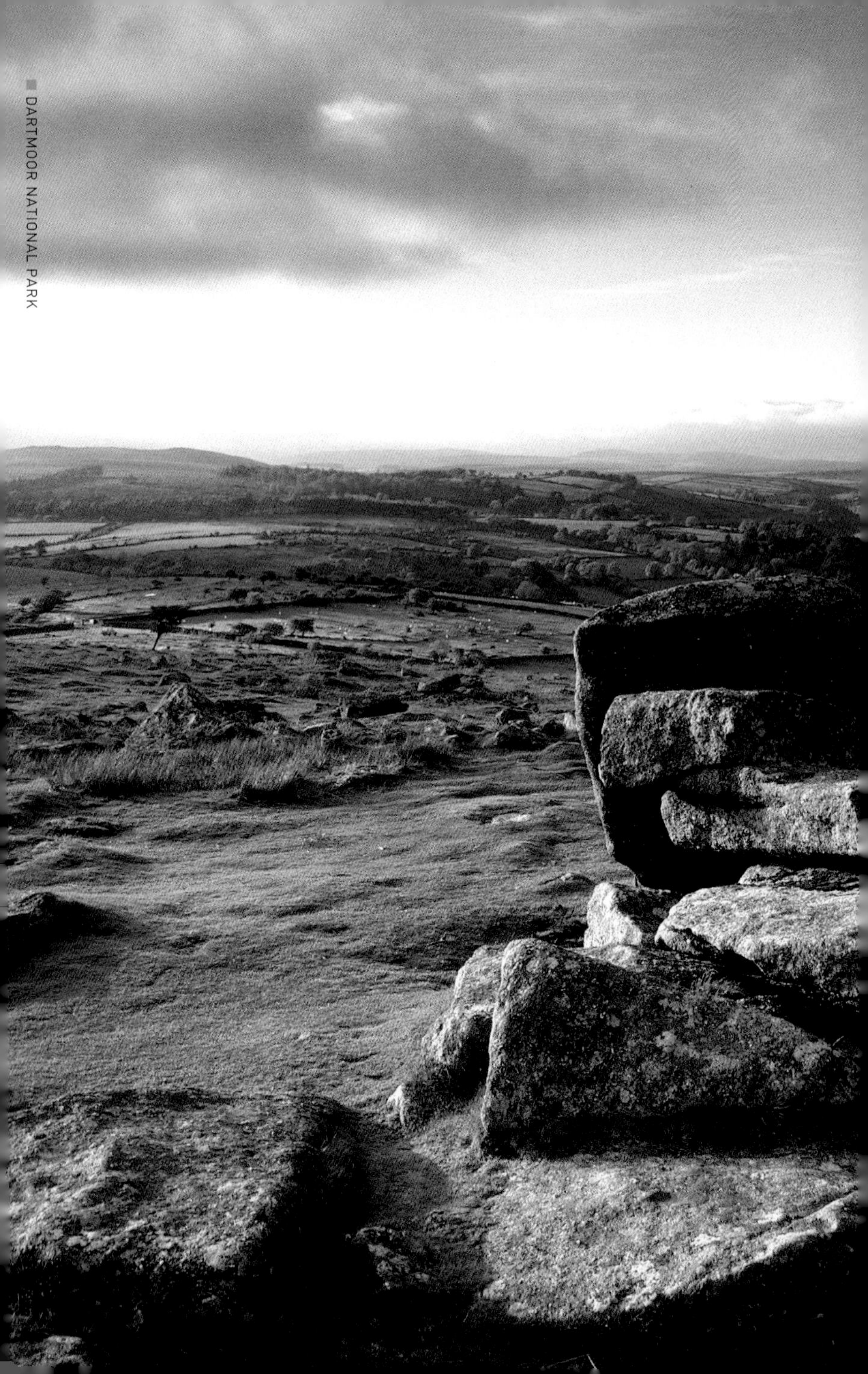

Dartmoor & Tamar Valley

Dartmoor is southern England's last great wilderness, though you might not think so if you only visit the picturesque villages of Widecombe or Buckland, set among gentle, rolling hills. But the bracken- and heather-covered uplands, interrupted by stark and distinctive granite outcrops, are quite another world, with mysterious standing stones dating back at least 6,000 years. Medieval tin, lead and copper mining have also left their mark. The Tamar Valley is an Area of Outstanding Natural Beauty. You will get much more out of your trip by taking to the water, either along the River Tamar itself, or on a trip around Plymouth Sound.

3 Walk start point

3 Cycle start point

2 Tour start point

POSTBRIDGE

TINSIDE LIDO, PLYMOUTH

Unmissable attractions

This part of Devon is packed with things to see and do. You can explore Plymouth's maritime heritage and then take a boat trip from the harbour; climb to the top of Smeaton's Tower and imagine what it would be like to be a lighthouse keeper; meander lazily through villages crammed with picture-postcard cottages with thatched roofs by car or bike; go walking or climbing on Dartmoor to see the famous tors, standing stones and stone circles; meet the ponies at the Dartmoor Pony Heritage Trust Centre or learn about monastic life at Buckfast Abbey.

4

5

1 Smeaton's Tower, Plymouth
For panoramic views of Plymouth Sound, climb to the top of this classic red-and-white striped lighthouse.

2 Buckland in the Moor
If you were to close your eyes and imagine an idyllic country village you would very probably imagine a place like Buckland in the Moor. This face of rural Devon has appeared on countless calendars and biscuit tins simply because it is so perfect.

3 Dartmoor National Park
Large boulders and waterfalls make an exciting landscape at Becky Falls near Manaton – perfect for walks and exploration. There are three trails, ranging from gentle (and suitable for children) to one for the seriously fit, which includes a climb.

4 River Tamar
Brunel's Royal Albert Bridge, opened in 1859, straddles the River Tamar to connect Plymouth and Saltash in Cornwall. While you are in this area, if you can, get on the water, either on a boat trip or by hiring a canoe.

5 Saddle Tor
From a distance, the tor actually does resemble a saddle. Although not as high as Hay Tor, it is still popular with climbers and walkers for its challenging ascents and wonderful views.

ASHBURTON MAP REF SX7570

Ashburton is the largest settlement on Dartmoor, even though it has just 3,500 inhabitants. It is a handsome, well-to-do market town with some fine old gabled and slate-hung houses, but the most important building is the 15th-century church, a monument to the profits from tin and cloth, for which the town was known. During the tin boom Ashburton was one of Devon's four Stannary towns and Ashburton cloth even found its way as far as China. In later years iron mining added to the town's coffers. Today Ashburton basks in its former prosperity and has fine pubs and antiques shops.

There is a local museum in the town centre, with a good collection of Native American artefacts, but undoubtedly the main attraction in the area is the family-oriented River Dart Adventures with woodland and riverside walks, an adventure playground and a lake.

■ Insight

DARTMOOR LETTER BOXES

The first 'Dartmoor letter box' was established just over 5 miles (8km) northwest of Postbridge at Cranmere Pool, a peat bog which, in 1854, was virtually inaccessible. Someone put a bottle here so those who had made it could leave a calling card. Serious walkers responded in their droves. In 1894 another 'letter box' site appeared; clues and map references were given, and so a fad was born. Since then there have been several variations on the 'calling card' theme but today, more than 5,000 letter boxes later, a rubber stamp and inkpad provide proof of a visit. Any Dartmoor tourist information office will tell you how to search for letter boxes.

BOVEY TRACEY MAP REF SX8178

Bovey Tracey is a pleasant small market town which bills itself as the Gateway to Dartmoor, because of its location at the busy southeastern corner of the moor. It is definitely worth a stop to explore the woodland and riverside walks of the Parke Estate (National Trust), half a mile (800m) west of the town. Parke is also the headquarters of the Dartmoor National Park Authority.

Back in the centre of Bovey Tracey is the beautifully restored Riverside Mill building – never actually used as a mill. It was built in 1850 as stables and the waterwheel simply scooped water from the river to a cistern used by the stables and adjacent house. It now houses a showcase for the members of the Devon Guild of Craftsmen, who produce some of the finest contemporary arts and crafts in the country, including jewellery, textiles, prints, ceramics and furniture.

Nearby is the Teign Valley Glass and House of Marbles centre, a shop in the former Bovey Tracey Pottery buildings selling marbles, glassware, games and toys. This is a major wet-weather attraction but the real interest is in the free demonstrations of glass-blowing. Three museums on the site explain the history of the Bovey potteries, glass, board games and marbles.

Near Bovey Tracey are a number of tors – naturally formed granite rock towers, often weathered into strange shapes by the forces of erosion. Haytor Rocks are the most accessible; the 30-feet (9m) high Bowerman's Nose is the most curiously shaped, resembling a face in profile. According to one legend, it is a local man who defied the injunction to rest on the Sabbath, went out hunting and was turned to stone; another has it that he disturbed a coven of witches, who subsequently petrified him and his hounds (Hound Tor). Nearby lies the Hound Tor deserted medieval village, the scant remains of dwellings, stables and grain stores of farmsteads abandoned at the time of the Black Death in the 14th century.

BRENT TOR   MAP REF SX4780

The tiny church of St Michael de Rupe at Brent Tor, one mile (1.6km) southwest of North Brentor village, is dramatically situated 1,100 feet (335m) above sea level on a small, steep volcanic hillock. On a clear day, stunning views stretch as far as Plymouth Sound to the south and some 40 miles (64km) northwards to the hills of Exmoor. But look around and there is nothing, so why was a church built here?

There are the usual Dartmoor tales relating to mischief by the devil, but a more plausible theory is that the tor may have been the only land visible to a 12th-century seafarer who found himself out at sea and in distress. He vowed that should he survive he would dedicate a church on that particular spot, and so in 1130 Brent Tor was built.

Today's church, which dates mostly from the 15th century but which was restored in the 19th century, has walls just 10 feet (3m) tall. In order to survive the fearsome elemental lashing they receive in this exposed setting, they were built 3 feet (1m) thick from the same volcanic material as the tor.

BUCKFASTLEIGH

MAP REF SX7366

The old market town of Buckfastleigh lies in a lush wooded valley, bypassed by the A38 and by most visitors, who head for either the station or Buckfast Abbey. The station is home to the South Devon Railway, a gloriously nostalgic steam line that runs along a beautiful 7-mile (11.3km) stretch of the River Dart as far as Totnes. The station site is shared by the excellent Dartmoor Otters and Buckfast Butterflies. The former is a large 'rainforest' hot house where exotic rainbow-hued specimens have no qualms about gently landing on visitors (a sort of 'wings-on' experience!). The Otter Sanctuary is a quasi-natural habitat with unobtrusive observation points where you can quietly watch these graceful creatures swim and play. Both are serious conservation projects, successfully walking the thin line between entertainment and education.

There are more animals to see at Pennywell, an 80-acre (32ha) farm and wildlife centre just one mile (1.6km) to the south. The farm scores particularly well with its long list of daily events, which include bottle-feeding, hand-milking, falconry demonstrations, sheepdog trials, pony training, ferret racing and even 'worm charming'.

Should you eventually make it into the centre of Buckfastleigh, brave the 196 cobbled steps that climb up on the northeast side of town (near the car park) to the church. This 13th-century monument was destroyed by fire in 1992, but it's well worth coming up here for the view across the countryside.

Around Brent Tor

A climb up to the 13th-century Church of St Michael de Rupe at Brent Tor. Lying just inside the national park boundary, the strange natural formation of Brent Tor is a remnant of the mass of lava that poured out on to the seabed here over 300 million years ago, when the area was a shallow sea. This extraordinary landmark provides the perfect focus for a relaxing exploration of this quiet corner of west Devon.

Route Directions

1 Walk straight ahead from your car towards Brent Tor, which positively invites you to visit it. Where the lane bears right turn left along an unfenced lane (dead end sign). Go gently downhill to pass Blacknor Park (left), then a cattle grid. The lane becomes rocky before passing Wortha Mill and crossing the disused railway line.

2 The track runs steeply uphill, before levelling off. At the next T-junction of tracks turn left to pass South Brentor Farm and a lane on the right, and keep straight on

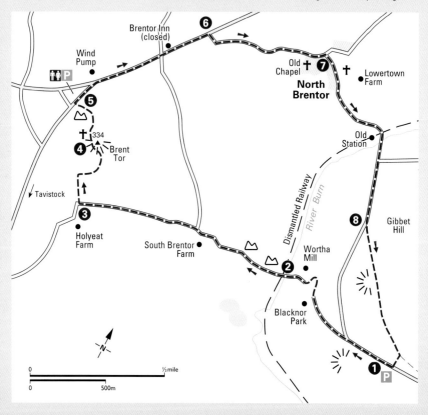

slightly uphill – under beech trees – to pass 'Hillside' on the left.

3 Pass Brennen Cottage (left); a few paces later the lane bends sharp left. Turn right through a gate and keep ahead up the right edge of the field on a permitted footpath. Turn right through a gate at the top, later bearing left going steeply uphill to reach Brent Tor church.

4 From the church door follow the path right then left to a gate, then downhill, bearing left to the road opposite the car park, where there are toilets and an information board.

5 Turn right along the road – take care – eventually passing the (closed) Brentor Inn on your left.

6 When you reach two white cottages on either side of the road, turn right down a tarmac lane signposted 'Brentor and Mary Tavy'. The lane runs gently downhill, with the moor rising steeply up behind the village ahead. This western edge of the moor is very different from the eastern side, where there is usually a long drive-in along wooded river valleys. At the edge of the houses

go straight on, keeping the old chapel on the right, until you reach the World War I memorial.

7 Turn right slightly downhill to pass the phone box, church and village hall. Follow the lane as it bears right to cross the old railway line. You can see the old station complete with platform canopy below you to the right.

8 Pass over the cattle grid on to the open moor, and up the lane. Where the lane bends right just past the gateway to Wortha Farm, cut left over the edge of Gibbet Hill on an indistinct grassy track. The lane leads back to the car, but this is a more pleasant route. Once over the crest of the hill you will see your route back to your car on the lane below to the right.

Route facts

DISTANCE/TIME 4.5 miles (7.2km) 2h

MAP OS Explorer 112 Launceston & Holsworthy

START Lay-by past cattle grid outside Mary Tavy on moorland road to North Brentor village, grid ref: SX 492800

TRACKS Tracks and green lanes, open fields and lanes

GETTING TO THE START The walk starts near Mary Tavy, which is about 5 miles (8km) north of Tavistock on the A386. Turn left at the garage in Mary Tavy, following the Brentor signs. In 0.5 mile (800m), cross a cattle grid on to open moorland. Park on the moorland to the right or in the small lay-by a little down the road on the left.

THE PUB Elephant's Nest, Horndon. Tel: 01822 810273 www.elephantsnest.co.uk

❶ One steep climb up to the summit of Brent Tor.

What to look for

Just southwest of Brent Tor is an enclosed area of mounds and depressions, all that remains of a 19th-century manganese mine, which was a major source of employment between 1815 and 1856. The manganese was used in the production of glass, bleach and steel, and was shipped out down the River Tamar from Morwellham Quay.

BUCKFAST ABBEY

MAP REF SX7467

Buckfast Abbey is one of the wonders of 20th-century England. The magnificent abbey church was built between 1907 and 1937 in the Cistercian style of the 12th century. This is remarkable enough until you learn that just four monks built the abbey and only one of them had any prior experience of masonry work. Were the abbey to acquire a veneer of age it would certainly be indistinguishable from its medieval forebear.

Today a small community of monks lead a life dedicated to prayer, work and study – not dissimilar to that of their counterparts who lived here from 1018 until the Dissolution in 1539. The monks returned in 1882, discovered the ruined medieval foundations and began the monumental task of totally rebuilding monastery and church. Not everything is new, however. Large parts of the medieval fabric of the South Gate and North Gate survived and have been restored, and the huge Guest Hall has also been renovated and now serves as an exhibition area.

There is an audio-visual presentation, an exhibition, the all-important tea rooms and the abbey shops, where you can stock up on Benedictine honey and the famous Buckfast Tonic Wine. These products are the most obvious way in which the abbey maintains financial self-sufficiency but another important source of income is its expertise in stained-glass windows. Over the last 50 years, three of the monks have designed and made windows for more than 150 churches as well as many private commissions. Just look at the abbey's own superb examples – particularly the great east window, the work of Father Charles – and you'll see why the windows are in such demand. About the only thing you cannot do is go inside the monastic quarters, but the exhibitions will satisfy most of your curiosity and there's always a friendly monk on hand to answer questions.

BUCKLAND ABBEY

MAP REF SX4867

Don't come to Buckland Abbey expecting to see hooded figures singing Gregorian Chants. If the Cistercians, who were evicted from here in 1539, came back tomorrow they would scarcely recognise the place. Following the Dissolution, the abbey was sold to Richard Grenville, a cousin of Walter Raleigh and the first in a line of illustrious seafarers to live here. His son Roger Grenville drowned aboard his famous command the *Mary Rose*, and his heir, another Richard Grenville, also met an untimely death aboard the *Revenge* in 1591.

By 1576, however, Grenville had completely changed the face of the abbey, demolishing many of the old monastic buildings, including the cloisters, building a Great Hall, and effectively converting it into a rather splendid Elizabethan mansion.

Francis Drake moved into Buckland Abbey in 1582 and stayed for 13 years, and it is this connection for which the house is best known. It remained in the direct Drake family line until 1794. The last occupant of Drake descendancy died in 1937 and then, following severe fire damage in 1938, the property passed into the care of the National Trust.

A few examples of delicate tracery and a stone corbel here and there are now the only obvious visible remains of the old abbey, and restoration since the fire has not been totally sympathetic. Nonetheless this is still an interesting house for visitors to explore, with many fine rooms, including the Great Hall, an atmospheric chapel containing several relics of the abbey's fabric, and a 16th-century kitchen. Among the fascinating Drake memorabilia are his drum, ship models, personal firearms, flags, medals and contemporary paintings.

Don't miss taking a leisurely stroll around the beautiful grounds and also popping into the craft workshops.

BUCKLAND IN THE MOOR
MAP REF SX7273

Although, you may not know it, you have probably already seen Buckland in the Moor. Its thatched cottages, nestling on the edge of the moor – it is the perfect English rural retreat – has starred on countless calendars, a thousand jigsaws and biscuit tins by the score. The other village building worth visiting is the 15th-century church – not because it is an outstanding example of Early English architecture (parts of it date back to the 12th century), or because of its Norman font (most visitors don't even see its superb screen). The big attraction is its clock face, on which the numerals have been replaced by the twelve letters M Y D E A R M O T H E R – a superb example of English sentimentality in a perfect setting.

■ Visit

THE GREAT BARN
The architectural highlight of the Buckland Abbey estate, and the only building that survived intact from the Cistercian period, is the 14th-century Great Barn, used by the monks for storage of crops, wool and hides. It has a superb arch-braced roof, measures 159 feet (48m) long by 32 feet (10m) wide and, to the ridge, 60 feet (18m) high, thus making it one of the largest barns in the country.

■ Visit

DRAKE'S DRUM
Buckland Abbey's most famous piece of Drake memorabilia is Drake's drum, rescued by his brother Thomas, when the great man died on the Spanish Main in 1596. Tradition has it that should England ever be in dire need and require the services of Drake again the drum will beat of its own accord.

■ Visit

BUCKLAND'S TEN COMMANDMENTS
Just to the east of Buckland in the Moor is Buckland Beacon, the West Country's answer to Mount Sinai, where you will find a version of the Ten Commandments carved in 1928, on a granite block, to mark Parliament's rejection of the proposed new Book of Common Prayer.

■ Insight

THE BUCKFAST BEE
Among apiarists (beekeepers) the name Buckfast is world famous, thanks largely to the pioneering work of Brother Adam, who devoted more than 70 years of his life to beekeeping at Buckfast Abbey, including breeding a new kind of bee. The Buckfast Bee is gentle, disease resistant, rarely swarms and provides excellent honey.

CANONTEIGN FALLS

MAP REF SX8383

Canonteign Falls is a privately owned beauty spot comprising lakes and waterfalls including the Lady Exmouth Falls, a sheer drop of 220 feet (67m) and the highest in England. Take the 1-mile (1.6km) trail through the woodland and you will find lakes and two more falls. This beautiful gorge scenery is partly man-made, first landscaped by Lady Exmouth in the 19th century. The view from the top of Lady Exmouth Falls is spectacular. Below, waterfowl swim on the lake and pond and a wetland nature reserve is stocked with more birds and waterplants. There is a shop and a café, exhibition, play area, paddocks with chickens, ducks, rabbits and donkeys, as well as a variety of exploratory trails and a large picnic area.

DARTMEET   MAP REF SX6773

Dartmoor's two principal rivers are the East Dart and the West Dart. Dartmeet, not surprisingly, is where they come together and is a popular beauty spot with a characteristic Dartmoor clapper bridge spanning the river. Like many such places in the area, it can get very busy in the high season, but a short walk – north along the river is a good bet – will soon take you through the valley where you can enjoy spectacular scenery away from the crowds.

DREWSTEIGNTON

MAP REF SX7391

The heart of Drewsteignton is a picture-postcard square with cob and thatch cottages, church and the Drewe Arms pub. From the square it's a short journey downhill to the 500-year-old Fingle Bridge and the start of the glorious Teign Gorge. Spring is wonderful, with carpets of daffodils and bluebells, and ornithologists will have a field day here. The walk ends after 6.5 miles (10.4km) at Steps Bridge, which like Fingle Bridge is an ever-popular and busy beauty spot.

The other major attraction here is Castle Drogo (National Trust), which, despite its Gothic name, dates from 1910 to 1930, and is in fact the last 'castle' to be built in England (by the foremost English architect of his day, Edwin Lutyens). Its exterior resembles a rather forbidding grey granite fortified country house – some critics have likened it to a prison – but the interior is far from spartan. The bare granite contrasts beautifully with rich tapestries, Spanish treasure chests and classic Oriental, French and English furnishings in an ingenious marriage of stately home and medieval fortress. There are also several Edwardian Arts and Crafts touches, and the kitchen, scullery and other 'downstairs' rooms are particular visitor favourites. The grounds have marvellous views over the Teign Valley.

■ Visit

DARTMOOR PONIES

At the Dartmoor Pony Heritage Centre at Brimpts Farm, near Dartmeet, you can get a close look at this delightful native breed. The Centre was set up by the DPH Trust in 2006 to educate visitors on the history and heritage of the native Dartmoor Pony, and also runs a scheme so you can adopt a Dartmoor Pony.

DARTMEET

Bridford and the Teign Valley

If you undertake this walk in early springtime, you can enjoy the sight of thousands of tiny wild daffodils crowding the river banks of the Teign, not to mention an exhilarating climb up Heltor Rock on route for Bridford and the very special Church of St Thomas Becket. Parts of the church possibly date from the 13th century but its main attraction is the carved and painted 16th-century rood screen.

Route Directions

1 From the car park cross the road, following the signs to the former youth hostel. Turn right up the concrete track, then left as signed towards the building; the path bears right, and is signed for Heltor Farm. The steep path leads uphill through delightful oak, then beech woodland. At the top of the wood cross a ladder stile as signed.

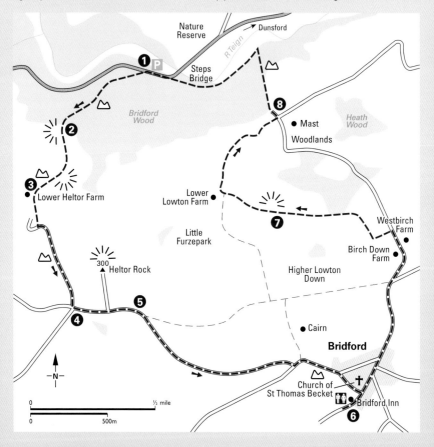

2 Follow wooden footpath posts straight up the field and through a small gate. Keep up the left edge of the next field; pass through a gateway and look to the left to see Heltor Rock.

3 At the end of the field turn left as signed through a wooden gate into a plantation; follow the path to meet a gate on to a lane. Turn left and walk uphill to meet a tarmac lane.

4 Turn left (signs for Bridford). After 200yds (183m) turn left over a stile up the narrow fenced permissive path to Heltor, from where you can enjoy an amazing panorama. Retrace your steps to the road and turn left.

5 After about 1 mile (1.6km) the lane bears left, then right, to reach the edge of Bridford. Turn right down a small steep lane signed 'Parish Hall & Church'. Follow the church wall path, down steps and right to find the Bridford Inn.

6 Turn left from the pub and follow the lane through the centre of the village. Take the fourth turning (Neadon Lane) on the right, by a telephone box. Just past where a bridleway joins (from the left) the lane dips

to the right, downhill; take the left fork ahead to pass Birch Down Farm on the right. Keep straight on at Westbirch Farm; turn left as signed to Lowton Farm on a fenced path, which bears right to a kissing gate; pass through and up the right edge of the next field to a stile in the top corner. Then cross over a tumbledown granite wall and carry straight on through an area of gorse bushes. Cross a stile by some beech trees.

7 Follow the fenced path along the top of two fields, and down a green lane to reach Lower Lowton Farm. Turn right as signed before the farm on a permissive bridlepath, which descends (with a stream, right) then rises to the next signpost; turn right for Steps Bridge down the narrow green lane, passing through a small gate. Continue down the deeply banked green lane until you reach a surfaced lane though a gate.

8 Turn left through the middle gate, signed 'Byway to Steps Bridge'. At the edge of Bridford Wood (by the National Trust sign) turn right following the footpath signposts. The path is fairly narrow and quite steep. Go left, then right, to cross a

Route facts

DISTANCE/TIME 5 miles (8km) 2h45

MAP OS Explorer 110 Torquay & Dawlish

START Free car park at Steps Bridge, grid ref: SX 803884

TRACKS Woodland paths, open fields and country lanes, 3 stiles

GETTING TO THE START Steps Bridge is well-signed, 9 miles (14.5km) west of Exeter, on the B3212 between Exeter and Moretonhampstead. Cross the bridge and go a little way up the hill and turn right into the car park.

THE PUB The Bridford Inn, Bridford. Tel: 01647 252436; www.bridfordinn.co.uk

❶ Some steep woodland paths on route.

track, keeping downhill. The path drops down steps then runs to the left, now high above the river to Steps Bridge where it meets the road opposite the former café. Turn left here to return to your car.

Woods around Lustleigh

This is a relatively gentle route (some steep sections) and will take you through pretty Lustleigh Cleave, via Wreyland's thatched farmhouses. It also runs through unspoiled Lustleigh – a charming (some would even say perfect) Devon village. The walk then heads steeply back uphill. For much of the walk you pass through Woodland Trust-managed Bovey Valley Woodlands, where you will see ancient trees and a rich variety of plantlife. You'll also wander along part of the east bank of the River Bovey.

Route Directions

1 From the parking area walk north up the lane (away from Lustleigh) and turn left up a narrow rocky path between the houses 'Logan Stones' and 'Grove', following bridleway signs 'Cleave for Water'. At the gate go straight ahead signed 'Hunters Tor' and climb steeply up to the top, where there are lovely views towards Hound Tor.

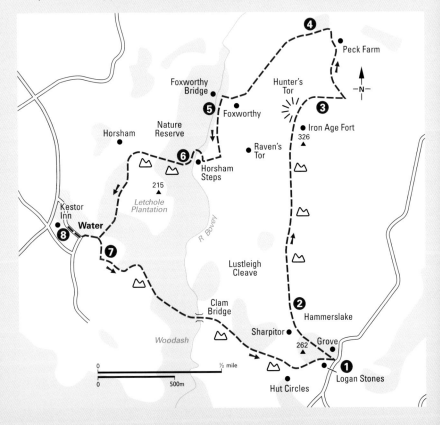

2 Turn right through oak woodland; eventually you reach open ground and follow the path straight on over the highest part of the ridge (1,063ft/324m) and across the remains of the Iron Age fort to reach Hunter's Tor.

3 Pass through the gate right of the tor and follow the signed path right downhill to meet another signed path left. Walk downhill through one gate, then immediately right through another and descend towards Peck Farm. Go through the gate to the left of the farm and straight on down the concrete drive.

4 Shortly after turn left through a gate signed 'Foxworthy Bridge' and continue along a wooded track to reach the beautiful thatched hamlet at Foxworthy; turn right.

5 At the path junction go left, signed 'Horsham'. Follow the track into mixed woodland through a gate. After 5 minutes or so follow signs right for 'Horsham for Manaton & Water', to the River Bovey. Follow the river bank left for a few paces to the crossing (on boulders) at Horsham Steps.
Note: If you are concerned about crossing Horsham Steps, don't turn left for 'Horsham' at Point 5, go right, down the drive, which crosses the river. Take the first footpath left and keep ahead until you rejoin the main route during Point 6; turn right uphill.

6 Cross over, taking care, and walk downstream to enter Bovey Valley Woodlands. Follow the path steeply uphill (the path avoiding Horsham Steps comes in right) and over a stile. Keep ahead to pass through a gate by pretty cottages (note the tree-branch porch). Keep straight on up the track, following signs for 'Water' through Letchole Plantation.

7 At the crossroads of tracks turn right ('Manaton direct') to meet the lane by the Water Mill. Take the second lane right to the Kestor Inn.

8 Retrace your steps to the crossroads. Go straight on downhill, signed 'Bovey Valley', to a split in the track. Keep left, eventually passing through a gate and continue down the steep, stony path. Cross the river on the bridge and proceed steeply uphill to the signpost. Go left, signed 'Lustleigh via Hammerslake', and left again at the next signpost (very steep). At the

next junction keep ahead uphill; where the path forks keep right to reach the gate; turn right down the rocky path back to the lane at the start.

Route facts

DISTANCE/TIME 4.75 miles (.7km) 2h30

MAP OS Explorer OL28 Dartmoor

START By side of lane at Hammerslake, grid ref: SX 775816

TRACKS Rough paths and woodland

GETTING TO THE START
Lustleigh is off the A382 between Moretonhampstead and Bovey Tracey, 4 miles (6.4km) northwest of Bovey Tracey. At the war memorial follow the road left to the church and then turn left, following the signs for Rudge. Turn right at Rudge Cross, signposted to Pethybridge. Keep straight on, passing two roads dropping to the left. The road soon widens where there are railings to the right and there are a few short areas to pull in close to the left of the road.

THE PUB The Cleave, Lustleigh.
Tel: 01647 277223;
www.thecleavelustleigh.com

❶ Some steep ascents and descents on rough paths and lanes are not suitable for very young children.

HOLNE   MAP REF SX7969

This pretty village 3 miles (4.8km) north of Buckfastleigh stands on the edge of Dartmoor. With a population of just 390, it nevertheless enjoys limited fame as a result of being the home of Charles Kingsley. The author of *The Water Babies*, *Westward Ho!* and *Hereward the Wake*, was born at Holne rectory in 1819.

It's a quiet place that doesn't attract many visitors and there are two charming refreshment options: the village pub, the 14th-century Church House Inn, which takes its name from the days when it (like other Church House Inns in Devon) brewed beer for the Church on feast days and enjoyed a close association with the clergy; and the village shop and tea room. The local church of St Mary the Virgin, dates from the 13th century.

■ Activity

CYCLING

Cycling in Devon, particularly on routes over Dartmoor, is a challenging prospect requiring a good level of fitness and a well-geared bicycle to cope with the steeply undulating terrain. There's gentler cycling on the sheltered southeastern edge of Dartmoor, where an intricate web of narrow rolling lanes explores the beautiful Dart Valley. For example, a leisurely day's cycle ride can link the picturesque villages of Buckland in the Moor, Holne and Widecombe in the Moor. The Plym Valley Trail on the western edge of the moor and the Granite Way (which goes from Okehampton to Lydford) both offer excellent cycling for families. Well-equipped off-road cycling enthusiasts can escape the crowds by venturing up on to the open moor.

IVYBRIDGE   MAP REF SX6356

This small, often overlooked town on the River Erme probably takes its name from the picturesque 13th-century humpback bridge which still spans the river today. There's nothing of great interest in the town but a walk north along the river is recommended. At Longtimbers Wood (a few minutes away) you will see some impressive granite pillars – all that remains of the viaduct that Brunel built in 1848 for the Great Western Railway.

Northwest of Ivybridge at Sparkwell is the popular Dartmoor Zoological Park. This entertaining zoo park, set in beautifully landscaped countryside, features birds of prey, lions, tigers and bears among its collection of around 250 species.

LUSTLEIGH   MAP REF SX7881

The focal point of this charming village is the 13th-century Church of St John, with a fine screen and some interesting memorials that recall 14th-century knights. Clustered around the centre of the village are a number of handsome old thatched buildings of late medieval origin, including the idyllic sunny-yellow Primrose Cottage tea rooms and the whitewashed 15th-century Cleave pub. Just 0.5 mile (800m) to the west of the village is the well-known beauty spot of Lustleigh Cleave, the steep-sided wooded valley of the River Bovey.

LYDFORD   MAP REF SX5185

This lovely unspoiled village is famous for its gorge and its castle, a plain, small, square ruined keep, built in 1195, which in medieval times gained notoriety as a prison court. The focus of the village is around the 16th-century oak-timbered Castle Inn, which was once the rector's home and contains a collection of 1,000-year-old pennies minted at Lydford during the reign of Ethelred II. Next door is the Church of St Petrock, mainly 15th century and in early medieval times the hub of the largest parish in England – anyone dying within its 50,000-acre (20,250ha) area of jurisdiction had to be buried here. Not surprisingly, St Petrock is famous for its graveyard where there are numerous interesting tombstones.

Just outside the village is the wooded valley of Lydford Gorge (National Trust), which stretches for 1.5 miles (2.4km) and in places measures up to 60 feet (18m) deep. A spectacular riverside walk ends at the 90-foot-high (27m) White Lady waterfall; en route the river has scooped a series of potholes where the water bubbles and boils, most notably in the thundering Devil's Cauldron.

MORWELLHAM QUAY

MAP REF SX4570

It's difficult to imagine today but between 1844 and 1859 this tranquil rural idyll deep in the Tamar Valley was the Klondike of its day, gripped by 'copper fever', when great deposits of copper ore were discovered locally. Morwellham Quay was the furthest navigable point on the River Tamar and several quays, a dock big enough to take six schooners and a 4.5-mile (7.2km) railway line were hurriedly built, followed by cottages to house the 200-strong community of miners, assayers and

■ Visit

NINE MAIDENS DANCING

The moors of Dartmoor National Park are littered with ancient standing stones, stone circles, stone rows and stone tombs. Many of these bizarre prehistoric remains are little understood even today and have attracted strange legends. One of the best-known stone formations is the Nine Maidens on Belstone Common, which lies just south of Okehampton. According to one version of the legend, these standing stones, which actually number 16 or 17 depending on your definition, come to life and dance on the Hunter's Moon (the first moon after the full moon nearest to the autumn equinox). Another version has it that they dance every day at noon. It's not so difficult to check the latter – just turn up at 12 o'clock and watch!

blacksmiths. But as the five mines were exhausted and river transport was sadly superseded by the railways, boom turned to bust. By 1880, after some 700,000 tons of copper and 70,000 tons of arsenic had been extracted, it was all over and the riverside port returned to its natural slumbers.

Morwellham Quay lay forgotten until 1970, when the Dartington Trust stepped in to restore it to its former glory; in 2006 the site was awarded World Heritage status. Today the quays and buildings are alive again with visitors exploring the fascinating infrastructure; visitors can board the *Garlandstone*, an old Tamar ketch moored at the quayside. The highlight of the visit is a trip deep into an actual copper mine aboard an electric tramway, but there is a lot more, particularly for children: horse-drawn carriage rides, costumes to try on, a ship to explore, demonstrations by blacksmiths and assayers, and a farm to wander around, so allow a whole day.

OKEHAMPTON MAP REF SX5995

Okehampton is the main town of north Dartmoor, with a range of shops for locals as well as for tourists, including a quaint Victorian covered arcade. Its main street, Fore Street, is dominated by the 14th-century tower of the Chapel of St James. At the opposite end of this street, tucked away in a charming cobbled courtyard adjacent to the White Hart Inn is the excellent Museum of Dartmoor Life. This is housed in an early 19th-century mill complete with working waterwheel and is bristling with many weird and wonderful old objects relating to Dartmoor crafts and industries.

A short walk from the centre are the ruins of Okehampton Castle (English Heritage), the largest castle in Devon. Parts date back to Norman times, though most of what remains today was built in the early 14th century by Hugh Courtenay, the Earl of Devon. Following the execution of the Earl in 1538 the castle was destroyed by Henry VIII. Today just enough remains to give a good idea of what it must have looked like. An entertaining personal stereo tour guides visitors around the buildings, at the same time outlining a supposed day in the life of the lady of the castle in medieval times. The setting, high on a hill overlooking the river and the beautiful woodlands which were once used as a royal deer park, is majestic.

PLYMOUTH MAP REF SX4754

Plymouth's seafaring legacy is legendary. The port was naturally blessed with one of Europe's finest deep-water anchorages and the patronage of Sir Francis Drake and Sir John Hawkins established its supremacy in the 16th century. It was, of course, from here in 1588 that Drake sailed to crush the Armada. In 1620 a more peaceable crew, the Pilgrim Fathers, set off from Plymouth aboard the *Mayflower* to make a new life in North America and to lay the foundation for New England.
In later years Captain Cook launched his voyages of discovery from here, while in the 19th century both colonists and convicts set sail to Australia from Plymouth. Recent history has not been so kind – the city was devastated during World War II and the centre has been completely rebuilt, but much of the old harbour area survived.

Start your visit on the grassy Hoe (it means 'high place' or 'hill') for a marvellous view over Plymouth Sound and its busy shipping lanes. Smeaton's Tower, the archetypal red-and-white lighthouse in the middle of the Hoe, was built in 1759 and once stood on the treacherous Eddystone Rocks, 14 miles (22.5km) out to sea. It was replaced in 1882 by a bigger lighthouse and was reassembled here. Climb to the top for great views. Just below the lighthouse is the wonderful and huge art deco Tinside Lido pool, open all day in the summer holidays (weather permitting).

Next to the Hoe is the Royal Citadel, a powerful star-shaped fortress built between 1666 and 1675. It is now home

to a commando regiment but guided tours in summer show the most interesting buildings, including the Royal Chapel of St Katherine (rebuilt in 1845). Just below the Citadel you'll find the National Marine Aquarium, one of the city's major visitor attractions and Britain's biggest aquarium, with more than 3,000 marine animals on display.

Keep walking down the hill and you will reach the Barbican, Plymouth's old harbour area. Several pleasure trips set off from here, the most popular being a one-hour tour around the dockyards. The oldest part of the Barbican is New Street, a cobbled street built in 1581, lined with timber-framed and jettied houses, including the atmospheric Elizabethan House, a rare surviving Tudor house which once belonged to a local sea captain. Also on New Street is a charming small Elizabethan garden. On Barbican Quay you will find the exciting Mayflower Centre, where you can learn about the history of the Barbican and experience the amazing story of the Pilgrim Fathers and the *Mayflower*.

In the modern centre of town, just a short walk north, some interesting old buildings survived the wartime bombing. On Finewell Street is the Prysten House (also known as Yogges House – visit by appointment only), a merchant's home and the oldest (1498) dwelling in the city, built around three sides of a galleried courtyard. Nearby is the Merchant's House, a classic four-storey Elizabethan building now housing a lively museum and a fully stocked apothecary's shop. The City Museum and Art Gallery has an outstanding collection of fine and decorative arts and holds temporary exhibitions throughout the year.

POSTBRIDGE MAP REF SX6579

Postbridge is classic Dartmoor. There isn't really a great deal here beyond a scattering of farms and cottages, the chapel and an inn – but Postbridge is a favourite starting and finishing point for Dartmoor walkers of all ages and abilities. Whether you want to join one of the numerous guided tours that depart from here or simply need information and maps in order to plan your own hike, you'll find helpful advice in the information office.

Postbridge's other claim to fame is its clapper bridge. This type of crossing is unique to Dartmoor and was built by medieval farmers and tin-workers in the 13th or 14th century. There are 30 such bridges on Dartmoor but the one at Postbridge is the best example of all. Its four huge slabs of granite, weighing up to 8 tons each and measuring up to 15 feet (4.5m) long by 7 feet (2m) wide, have been carefully placed over the East Dart on three granite piers, just like rough-hewn building pieces from a baby giant's construction kit. The adjacent road bridge dates from the 1780s.

PRINCETOWN MAP REF SX5873

Princetown is Dartmoor at its bleakest, greyest and grimmest. No wonder, then, that this spot was chosen for Dartmoor Prison. It was built in 1806 to house French prisoners captured during the Napoleonic Wars, and between 1812 and 1814 it confined Americans taken during the War of Independence. Conditions were grim and overcrowded and around 1,000 Frenchmen and Americans died here from jail fever. From 1816 to 1850 the prison stood empty, until it was revived for criminal offenders. Displays at the Prison Heritage Centre, which is housed in converted prison stables, give a fascinating history of Dartmoor Prison.

At 1,400 feet (427m) above sea level, Princetown claims to be the highest town in England (though in fact it is very little more than a village). However, its altitude makes it the natural centre of the 'High Moorland' and the excellent National Park Visitor Centre and information point in the early 19th-century Old Duchy Hotel. Princetown hosts the Dartmoor Brewery, home to the appropriately named Jail Ale.

SALTRAM HOUSE

MAP REF SX5155

Saltram House, which is managed by the National Trust, is Plymouth's very own grand country mansion; in fact it is the largest house in Devon. It lies just within the city boundary (unfortunately close to the busy A38), yet its setting, high above the River Plym in 300 acres (121ha) of beautiful parkland, is bucolic. The house is a classic 18th-century mansion which was then enlarged and remodelled for the Parker family in 1740 from a 16th-century house. It is remarkable for its state of preservation and is also a showcase for the work of both Robert Adam and Joshua Reynolds. Adam's magnificent interior plasterwork and decoration are most prominent in the saloon and in the dining room

■ Visit

A GUNPOWDER FACTORY

One mile (1.6km) southwest of Postbridge on the B3212 is Powder Mills, built in 1844 as a gunpowder factory. Demand for local quarry blasting provided a healthy market until the invention of dynamite in 1867 and the factory closed in the 1890s. Today only its chimneys remain, but a craft gallery and pottery workshops have now been set up in the cottages which were once home to the gunpowder factory workers.

■ Insight

REYNOLDS AT SALTRAM

From 1770 onwards the famous portrait artist Joshua Reynolds came to Saltram House on a regular basis, becoming firm friends with Lord Boringdon and his family and undertaking more commissions from them than from any other of his regular customers. Saltram still has many of the artist's paintings on display, including a portrait of his patron, which is considered unique. During his frequent visits to the house, Reynolds liked nothing better than a day's hunting or shooting, unless it was to partake in one of the gambling parties organised by Lord Boringdon.

(completed 1768). Reynolds, who was the most fashionable English portrait artist of his day, was a master at the local grammar school and a personal friend of the Parker family. As a result of this close connection, 14 full-length portraits hang in the house. The artistic tradition lives on in the chapel, which houses a gallery of West Country art. The Great Kitchen is another highlight of the house, while the gardens are also well worth exploring on a fine day.

Dartmoor and the Tamar Valley

This drive skirts the northwestern edge of Dartmoor before climbing on to its most spectacular, granite-dotted open moorland. From the most southerly point of the drive, the return is through the beautiful countryside of the Tamar Valley. The drive begins in Okehampton, which has an attractive wide main street, flanked by some fine old buildings. Just off the main street is a cobbled courtyard housing a Victorian tea room, a tourist information centre and the Museum of Dartmoor Life. The impressive ruins of Okehampton Castle are on the southwestern edge of the town.

Route Directions

1 From the traffic lights in the town centre take the B3260, signposted 'Tavistock'. In 3 miles (4.8km) cross a road bridge and turn right on to the A30, signposted 'Launceston'. In 1 mile (1.6km) take the A386, signed 'Tavistock' and 'Plymouth', and continue for 9 miles (14.5km) to Mary Tavy.
Mary Tavy, a peaceful village now, was once famous for its tin- and copper-mining industry. The preserved remains of Wheal Betsy engine house are passed just before reaching the village.

2 Continue for 3.75 miles (6km), with fine views of Dartmoor on the left, to reach Tavistock.
One of four stannary towns around the moor, Tavistock, although it is much older, is essentially a product of 19th-century prosperity. It has a thriving covered market – the town was granted a market

charter in 1105 – and bustling main street and is one of the most attractive 'working' towns in the county.

3 Just before reaching the town centre, turn left onto the B3357, which is signposted 'Princetown'. The road soon climbs onto open moorland with huge outcrops of granite all around, including Cox Tor on the left.

4 In 6.5 miles (10.4km) turn right, signed 'Princetown', and continue for 1 mile (1.6km) to Princetown, with sombre views down over the prison to the left. Pass the Dartmoor Prison Museum and the excellent National Park Visitor Centre, then turn right at a roundabout on to the B3212, which is signed 'Yelverton, Plymouth', a road which has some of the most spectacular views on the moor. In 6.25 miles (10.1km) reach a roundabout and take the first exit on to the A386,

signposted 'Plymouth'.
In half a mile (800m) turn right, signposted 'Crapstone, Buckland Monachorum, Milton Combe', with brown tourist signs to The Garden House and Buckland Abbey. In 1.25 miles (2km) detour left to visit Buckland Abbey. This splendid former monastic foundation later became the home of Sir Francis Drake.

5 Continue on the main route, passing The Garden House in half a mile (800m) on the right. In another half mile (800m) turn left, signposted 'Milton Combe' and 'Bere Alston'. After a further half mile (800m) turn right, signposted 'Bere Alston', descending through a delightful wooded valley to cross the River Tavy at a picturesque stone bridge, following signs for 'Bere Alston'. Ascend a 1-in-5 (20%) hill and in 2 miles (3.2km) turn right, signed 'Gulworthy'

and 'Tavistock'. In another 2.5 miles (4km) detour left for a mile (1.6km) to visit Morwellham Quay.
This once thriving copper mine and port has been accurately renovated and restored to form a splendid open-air museum, staffed by craftsmen and other workers in period costume.

6 On the main route continue for 1.5 miles (2.4km) to meet the A390. Keep ahead over the roundabout, signed 'Chipshop', 'Lamerton' and 'Milton Abbot'. In 4.75 miles (7.7km) cross the B3362, then in 1.25 miles (2km) turn right, signposted 'Brentor'. In a further mile (1.6km) continue straight on at crossroads, signed 'Brentor'. In 1.5 miles (2.4km) reach the car park for Brent Tor Church on the right. Perched atop a high grassy mound with great rocks strewn all around, the church has panoramic views from all sides.

7 Shortly after the car park turn left, signed 'Brentor' and 'Lydford'. In 3 miles (4.8km) pass the first entrance to Lydford Gorge on the left. This beautiful wooded gorge, owned by the National Trust, has a 3.5-mile (5.7km) walk with a waterfall at one end and the spectacular Devil's

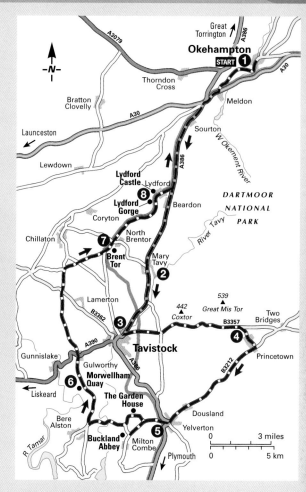

Cauldron at the other end of the route.

8 Continue for 1.5 miles (2.4km) to reach Lydford Castle, a great square stone keep which dates from 1195 – at one time a gaol. In 0.75 mile (1.2km) turn left on to the A386, signposted 'Okehampton'. In 5.75 miles (9.2km) turn right on to the A30, signed 'Okehampton' and 'Exeter'. In half a mile (800m) turn left, signed 'Okehampton', and follow the B3260 for 2.5 miles (4km) back to the town centre.

The Princetown Railway

There's a long history of granite quarrying on Dartmoor. It began around 1820 at Haytor Quarry and (in direct competition) at Swelltor and Foggintor. Look towards Foggintor (Point 3) and you'll see various ruined buildings: as well as cottages there was also a chapel used as a school. The old quarry workings are now flooded and provide a peaceful picnic spot. This is a tough ride through the wilds of Dartmoor, along the old route of the Princetown to Yelverton railway.

Route Directions

1 Turn left out of the car park along the rough road. Just past the fire station (left) bear left as signed (disused railway/Tyrwhitt Trail) on a narrow fenced path, which bears right. Go through the gate. The path widens to a gritty track and passes a coniferous plantation (right).

2 Suddenly you're out in the open on a long embankment, looking towards the forests around Burrator Reservoir ahead right, below Sheeps Tor and Sharpitor (right). Continue along the contours of the hill – it's quite rough – and as you progress look ahead left to the railway winding its way towards Ingra Tor. This is the old Plymouth and Dartmoor railway line, the brainchild of Sir Thomas Tyrwhitt, who was a friend of and private secretary to the Prince Regent. Originally a tramway with horse-drawn

wagons, it opened in 1823. The line was part of Tyrwhitt's plans to exploit the area's natural resources (granite), while at the same time enabling materials such as coal and lime to be brought to Princetown more easily. The Princetown Railway Company (a subsidiary of the Great Western Railway) took it over in 1881; it reopened as a steam railway in 1883, but was not profitable and closed in 1956. However, it makes a great cycle track.

3 Reach the edge of Foggintor Quarry (right), with Swelltor Quarry on the hill ahead; a track crosses the trail. The site of King Tor Halt (1928), from where a siding led to Foggintor, is nearby. Keep straight ahead, almost immediately taking the left fork (the track becomes grassier). Look right towards the spoil heaps of Foggintor Quarry. Follow the track on

Route facts

DISTANCE/TIME 5 miles (8km) 1h45

MAP OS Explorer OL28 Dartmoor

START Princetown car park (contributions), grid ref: SX 588735

TRACKS Rocky former railway track and one particularly steep and rough section

GETTING TO THE START Princetown lies on the B3212 between Two Bridges and Yelverton. From Two Bridges, turn right in the middle of the town; from Yelverton, turn left (National Park Visitor Centre on the corner), following signs for the car park.

CYCLE HIRE Runnage Farm, Postbridge (plus camping barn). Tel: 01822 880222; www.runnagecampingbarns.co.uk

THE PUB Dartmoor Inn, near Princetown. Tel: 01822 890340

❶ Only suitable for older children with mountain bikes.

– look left towards Merrivale Quarry (Dartmoor Inn is just out of sight below) – and try to spot the Bronze Age Merrivale stone rows. Follow the track as it bears left round the hill (below King's Tor Quarry), to enjoy views right over Vixen Tor, almost 1,040ft (317m) high, home to one of the moor's most evil folklore characters, the witch Vixana.

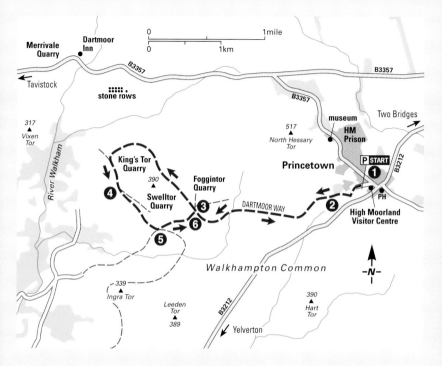

Pass through a cutting – there is another branch also that joins right – and keep cycling on to another fork.

4 Keep right along the lower track; views change again, with the wooded Walkham Valley below right and – on a good day – the sparkling waters of Plymouth Sound in the distance. About 50yds (46m) beyond the fork look left to see a pile of dressed stone on the upper track: 12 granite corbels, cut in 1903 for work on London Bridge, but excess to requirements.

Pass the spoil heaps of Swelltor Quarry; the track is now fenced on the right, with views ahead to the bridge en route for Ingra Tor.

5 Where the track starts to curve sharp right, turn left opposite an old gate. Push your bike up a rough, rocky track to regain the outward route near Foggintor Quarry.

6 Turn right and make your way bumpily back to Princetown. The building of the infamous prison in 1806 – originally for French prisoners

from the Napoleonic Wars – was also down to Thomas Trywhitt. Since 1850 it has been a civilian establishment.

STICKLEPATH MAP REF SX6494

'Stickle' means steep in Anglo-Saxon and the steep path in question once ran down from the village to the River Taw. The Taw at this point flows swiftly off the moor and during the Industrial Revolution its energy was harnessed by several waterwheels in Sticklepath to grind corn, to spin wool and to power a small factory making agricultural tools.

This small factory, now known as the Finch Foundry and managed by the National Trust, survived from 1814 right up to 1960. It was closed for a brief period but was later was restored to partial working order and reopened as a museum of industrial history. Though this may sound pretty dull fare, it's quite a sight when the sluices are opened. The powerful waterwheels start turning and these drive cogs and pulleys in the most delightful Heath Robinson fashion in order to set the ancient machinery in motion. There are three wheels: one either hammers the raw iron 'bloom' to make wrought iron or powers metal-cutting shears; another grinds or polishes metal or cuts wood;

■ Activity

STICKLEPATH CYCLE ROUTE

This 30-mile (48km) circular route from Sticklepath skirts the northern fringes of Dartmoor and follows the Rivers Taw and Okement, passing through Hatherleigh and Okehampton. The route takes in pretty villages with stocks and blacksmiths and passes old manor houses. The West Devon Sticklepath Cycle Route, the Tarka Trail cycleway and the Mid-Torridge Link form a complete cycle route from Dartmoor to the north Devon coast.

the third powers a fan which acts as a bellows to heat the furnaces and forges. The foundry isn't just a study in industrial engineering, however. Its working practices and its relationship to the small village also make it an interesting study in social history, not to mention alternative energy, and these aspects too are explained to visitors.

TAVISTOCK MAP REF SX4874

Tavistock today is little more than a pleasant market town but it was once home to the most powerful abbey in southwest England. Parts of the Benedictine structure still stand, the abbey gateway has been incorporated into the town hall and opposite its infirmary dining hall is now a chapel. Betsey Grimbal's Tower, the abbey's west gatehouse, stands next to the Bedford Hotel and part of the cloisters is retained in the yard of the handsome 15th-century Church of St Eustace.

The town's second great period of wealth came in the 13th century with tin mining, when Tavistock became the largest of Devon's four stannary towns. By the time the supply of tin had been exhausted in the 17th century, a thriving cloth trade was prospering in Tavistock and then along came the great 'copper rush' of the mid- to late 19th century when a rich lode was discovered locally. As boom turned to bust Tavistock's population dropped from 9,000 to 6,000 and the market town readjusted to its original role. Today Tavistock's famous Victorian covered Pannier Market is well worth a visit. Tavistock also hosts a fortnightly farmers' market.

Tavistock's most famous son is Francis Drake, who was born in 1542 at Crowndale Farm just south of the town. There's nothing to see there, but there is a fine statue at the end of Plymouth Road in the town centre. This is the original (cast in 1883) of the famous one on Plymouth Hoe, which is a copy.

WIDECOMBE IN THE MOOR
MAP REF SX7176

This picturesque Dartmoor village, set among rolling green hills, surrounded by high granite-strewn ridges, really does attract thousands of visitors in summer and at peak times its natural charm can be somewhat overwhelmed. However, despite the tea rooms and tourist paraphernalia, little has changed here over the centuries. The famous fair is still celebrated on the second Tuesday in September, but its remit has grown from the simple horse-trading fair it once was to accommodate the coachloads who now descend upon it.

The spire of the local Church of St Pancras, 'the Cathedral of the Moors', is a landmark for miles. The church was built in the 14th century and enlarged over the course of the next two centuries. It is more than 100 feet (30.5m) in length, and its most notable feature is its fine roof bosses. Look out for the sign of the three rabbits. Ironically this docile emblem, linked to alchemy, was adopted by the tin miners. A less docile crowd you could never wish to meet; Sir Walter Raleigh, in his capacity as Warden of the Stannaries (tin mines), described them as 'the roughest and most mutinous men in England'.

The adjacent Church House (National Trust) dates back to 1537, when it was a brewhouse. It was also a rest house for outlying farming families who had a very long distance to travel to Widecombe for services. It later became almshouses, then a school and now serves as the village hall. It also hosts the monthly village market. The adjacent Sexton's Cottage is now a National Trust and Dartmoor information centre and shop.

If you want to drink in the real atmosphere of Widecombe the pleasant main village pub, the Old Inn, dates back to the 14th century, but it has been much altered and is often packed with visitors. Walk a little way past the church and you'll find the ancient Rugglestone Inn.

YELVERTON MAP REF SX5267

The village of Yelverton itself is of little interest, though it is home to unusual attractions, such as the Yelverton Paperweight Centre, which displays more than 800 of these curious heavy glass blobs. A mile (1.6km) east is the delightful, little-visited village of Meavy, with a whitewashed pub, a medieval church and a manor house that once belonged to the Drake family.

Further east the rocky crag of Sheepstor crowns the skyline. The tiny, pretty hamlet here looks down over the Burrator Reservoir. Water from here supplies Plymouth. West of Yelverton, at Buckland Monachorum, is the Garden House with a walled garden with an enormous range of colourful plants. The house is also open in the summer to garden visitors for lunch and afternoon tea.

■ TOURIST INFORMATION CENTRES

Okehampton
White Hart Courtyard.
Tel: 01837 53020;
www.okehamptondevon.co.uk

Plymouth
Mayflower Centre, Barbican.
Tel: 01752 306630;
www.plymouthcity.co.uk

Tavistock
Bedford Square.
Tel: 01822 612938;
www.tavistock-devon.co.uk

Dartmoor National Park Authority
Parke, Bovey Tracey.
Tel: 01626 832093;
www.dartmoor-npa.gov.uk
www.virtuallydartmoor.org.uk

National Park Visitor Centre
Old Duchy Hotel,
Princetown.
Tel: 01822 890414

COMMUNITY INFORMATION CENTRES

Ashburton
By car park.
Tel: 01364 653426; www.
ashburton.org/infocentre

Bovey Tracey
Lower car park.
Tel: 01626 832047;
www.boveytracey.gov.uk

Buckfastleigh
Valiant Soldier.
Tel: 01364 644522;
www.buckfastleigh.org

Haytor
Lower car park.
Tel: 01364 661520

Ivybridge
The Watermark.
Tel: 01752 892220;
www.ivybridgedevon.co.uk

Moretonhampstead
The Square.
Tel: 01647 440043; www.
moretonhampstead.co.uk

Postbridge
Car park on B3212.
Tel: 01822 880272

■ PLACES OF INTEREST

Buckfast Abbey
Buckfastleigh. Tel: 01364
645500; www.buckfast.org.uk

Buckland Abbey
Buckland Monachorum.
Tel: 01822 853607;
www.nationaltrust.org.uk

Castle Drogo
Drewsteignton.
Tel: 01647 433306;
www.nationaltrust.org.uk

City Museum and Art Gallery
Drake Circus, Plymouth.
Tel: 01752 304774; www.
plymouthmuseum.gov.uk

Dartmoor Otters and Buckfast Butterflies
Buckfastleigh.
Tel: 01364 642916; www.
ottersandbutterflies.co.uk

Dartmoor Zoololgical Park
Sparkwell. Tel: 01752 837645

Devon Guild of Craftsmen
Riverside Mill, Bovey Tracey.
Tel: 01626 832223

The Garden House
Buckland Monachorum,

Yelverton. Tel: 01822 854769;
www.thegardenhouse.org.uk

Lydford Gorge
Lydford (off A386).
Tel: 01822 820441;
www.nationaltrust.org.uk

Mayflower Centre
Barbican Quay, Plymouth.
Tel: 01752 306330;
www.plymouthcity.co.uk

Merchant's House Museum
33 St Andrews Street,
Plymouth. Tel: 01752 304774;
www.plymouthmuseum.gov.uk

Morwellham Quay
Morwellham.
Tel: 01822 832766/833808;
www.morwellham-quay.co.uk

Museum of Dartmoor Life
West Street, Okehampton.
Tel: 01837 52295;
www.museumofdartmoorlife.
eclipse.co.uk

National Marine Aquarium
The Barbican, Plymouth.
Tel: 01752 220084;
www.nationalaquarium.co.uk

Okehampton Castle
Okehampton.
Tel: 01837 52844;
www.english-heritage.org.uk

Royal Citadel
The Hoe, Plymouth.
Tel: 01752 255629;
www.ecastles.co.uk

Saltram House
Plympton. Tel: 01752 333503;
www.nationaltrust.org.uk

Smeatons Tower
Plymouth. Tel: 01752 304774;
www.plymouth.gov.uk

South Devon Railway
Buckfastleigh.
Tel: 0845 345 1420; www.
southdevonrailway.org.uk

■ FOR CHILDREN

Brimpts Farm
Dartmeet. Includes Dartmoor
Pony Heritage Trust.
Tel: 01364 631450;
www.brimptsfarm.co.uk/
www.dpht.co.uk

Dartmoor Railway
Okehampton.
Tel: 01837 55164;
www.dartmoorrailway.co.uk

Miniature Pony Centre
Moretonhampstead.
Tel: 01647 432400; www.
miniatureponycentre.com

Pennywell Farm
Buckfastleigh.
Tel: 01364 642023;
www.pennywellfarm.co.uk

■ SHOPPING

Bovey Tracey
Farmers' market, alternate
Sats.

Buckfastleigh
Farmers' market, Thu.

Ivybridge
Country market, Fri.

Okehampton
Farmers' market, 3rd Sat.

Plymouth
Farmers' market, 4th Sat.

Tavistock
Pannier Market, Tue–Sat.
Farmers' market, 2nd and
4th Sat.

LOCAL SPECIALITIES
Crafts
The Devon Guild of
Craftsmen, Bovey Tracey.
Tel: 01626 832223;
www.crafts.org.uk

Country Cheeses
Pannier Market, Tavistock.
Tel: 01822 615035;
www.countrycheeses.co.uk

Powdermills Pottery
Postbridge.
Tel: 01822 880263;
www.powdermillspottery.com

**PERFORMING ARTS IN
PLYMOUTH**

Barbican Theatre
Castle Street.
Tel: 01752 267131;
www.barbicantheatre.co.uk

Plymouth Arts Centre
38 Looe Street.
Tel: 01752 206114;
www.plymouthartscentre.org

Theatre Royal/Drum Theatre
Royal Parade.
Tel: 01752 267222;
www.theatreroyal.com

■ SPORTS & ACTIVITIES

ANGLING
Fly fishing
Drakelands Trout Fishery,
Hemerdon, nr Plymouth.
Tel: 01752 344691
Milemead Fisheries, Mill Hill,
Tavistock. Tel: 01822 610888;
www.milemeadfisheries.com

**COUNTRY PARKS, FORESTS
& NATURE RESERVES**
Managed by Devon Wildlife

Trust or Forestry Commission
England or English Nature:
see page 152.

CYCLE HIRE
Ashburton
Bigpeaks Mountain Bike
Centre. Tel: 01364 654080;
www.bigpeaks.com

Sourton
Devon Cycle Hire.
Tel: 01827 861141 or
01822 615014;
www.devoncyclehire.co.uk

HORSE-RIDING
Poundgate
Babeny Farm Stables.
Tel: 01364 631296;
www.babenystables.co.uk

Widecombe in the Moor
Shilstone Rocks Riding
Centre. Tel: 01364 621281;
www.dartmoorstables.com

SAILING
Plymouth
Plymouth Sailing School.
Tel: 01752 493377;
www.plymsail.demon.co.uk

■ ANNUAL EVENTS &
CUSTOMS

Okehampton
Okehampton Show, Aug.
Carnival, mid-Oct.

Plymouth
Plymouth Navy Days, biennial
event, Aug Bank Hol.

Tavistock
Goosey Fair, mid-Oct.

Widecombe in the Moor
Widecombe Fair, 2nd Tue
in Sep.

Tea Rooms

Dartmoor Tearooms & Café
Moretonhampstead TQ13 8NL
Tel: 01647 441116; www. dartmoortearooms.co.uk
Delightful, cosy licensed tea room in the heart of this little moorland town, with a huge range of teas and coffees. Huge home-made scones, delicious cakes (lemon and blueberry drizzle, rich chocolate brownie, carrot cake, French apple and blackcurrant tartlet) all served with a smile in an elegant setting. Also soups, hot-filled baguettes and light lunches, and ingredients sourced locally.

Ullacombe Farm Shop and Barn Café
Bovey Tracey TQ13 9LL
Tel: 01364 661341
Once a small stall selling homegrown produce, now an excellent farm shop and café serving a good range of delicious dishes; many of the ingredients are grown on site. Soups and salads, pasties, pies, quiches, Sunday lunches and – of course – excellent cream teas and home-made cakes. A relaxed spot with a woodburner, sofas, newspapers to read, and farm animals to visit.

Brimpts Farm
Dartmeet, Dartmoor PL20 6FG
Tel: 01364 631450; www.brimptsfarm.co.uk
Brimpts Farm has a spectacular setting above Dartmeet and overlooking Yar Tor. Their cream teas have been justly renowned since 1913; scones and home-made cakes follow farmhouse recipes and the menu includes dishes made from fresh local produce.

Pubs

Warren House Inn
Postbridge PL20 6TA
Tel: 01822 880208; www.warrenhouseinn.co.uk
An open fire that hasn't gone out since 1845 is one of the claims to fame of this pub on Dartmoor. Popular with walkers, its views across the moor are stunning. The menu ranges from rabbit pie and Dartmoor lamb to West Country cheeses, pasties and vegetarian dishes.

The Bearslake Inn
Lake, nr Sourton EX20 4HQ
Tel: 01837 861334; www.bearslakeinn.com
This 13th-century thatched longhouse is really worth a visit, for the surroundings and for the food. Extensively renovated, the pub retains a genuine 'old' feel, and has a large garden with a stream. All their produce is sourced from the West Country, with specials such as blue cheese chicken, steak and kidney pie, and good vegetarian options.

The Royal Oak Inn
Meavy PL20 6PJ
Tel: 01822 852944; www.royaloak.inn.org.uk
A traditional 15th-century pub on the village green near a huge oak, said to have once provided a hiding place for King Charles. Warm, friendly, with a real 'local' feel, serving hearty fare: local cheeses, Dartmoor steak and Jail Ale pie, sticky toffee pudding. The pub participates in the Meavy Oak Fair, held each June.

The Elephant's Nest Inn
Horndon, Mary Tavy, Tavistock PL19 9NQ
Tel: 01822 810273; www.elephantsnest.co.uk
A pub since the mid-19th century, the building dates from the 16th century, when it accommodated miners. There's a beamed bar with an open fire, two dining rooms and a pretty garden. The interesting menu includes beetroot and blue cheese *antipasti,* home-made fish pie and the unusually named, 'Elephant burger'.

South Coast

In 1983 the resorts of Brixham, Torquay and Paignton were relaunched as the English Riviera, an exotic, yet still very English alternative to going abroad. Torquay comes closest to achieving the sophisticated image; Paignton is more kiss-me-quick than *je ne sais quoi*, while Brixham remains an unspoilt fishing port. The South Hams is, however, a very different world – an agricultural region studded with small villages. The countryside is beautiful, especially along the River Dart and around the Kingsbridge estuary. In Totnes and Dartmouth Devon has two of England's most charming small towns.

6 Walk start point

BRIXHAM

TOTNES CASTLE

Unmissable attractions

This is probably the busiest and most touristy part of the county, and with good reason. The mild climate and numerous beaches mean that this area can have quite a continental feel. There are the attractions of Torquay's beaches and the town itself, as well as the chance to learn how to sail at one of the sailing schools at Dartmouth, Teignmouth, Torquay or Salcombe. If leaving the land behind is not for you, try tackling part of the South West Coast Path, which takes in all of the coastal resorts as well as the lighthouse at dramatic Start Point.

1 Kingsbridge Estuary
The Rivermaid Ferry links Kingsbridge with Salcombe on the other side.

2 Brixham
A replica of the *Golden Hind* dominates the harbour in this pretty village.

3 Torquay
Clear water and clean beaches make Torquay's beach huts a highly sought after commodity.

4 Dartmouth & River Dart
People come here for the cute cobbled streets, colourful houses and the chance to go sailing.

5 Rickham Sands
This beach is one of the best in the region.

6 Start Point
The South West Coast path passes by Start Point.

BERRY POMEROY CASTLE

MAP REF SX8261

Berry Pomeroy is one of Devon's best-known castles, famous for its romantic, ruined, ivy-dripping appearance and for its many ghosts. Certainly many of the Pomeroys, who settled here after the Norman Conquest, met violent deaths, as did the builder of much of the present castle, Edward Seymour, who was executed in 1552, shortly after he had acquired Berry Pomeroy. His designs were never completed, the castle was partially destroyed in a fire and by the mid-18th century it was deserted. English Heritage are the custodians.

It's an unusual design, being a mansion within a castle. Inside the gatehouse and massive curtain wall are the ruins of a great Tudor house, with a hall nearly 50 feet (15m) long. The earliest parts of the castle go back to the 14th century and a 15th-century fresco also remains from the Pomeroy period. The other delight of visiting Berry Pomeroy is its superb situation, high on a wooded hillside overlooking a glorious deep valley and stream.

Among the ghosts said to inhabit the ruins of Berry Pomeroy Castle are a daughter of the castle and her secret paramour, who also happened to be an enemy of her family. They were discovered in each other's arms one night by her brother, who killed them both, so that they are now destined to remain just out of reach of true happiness for eternity.

BRIXHAM   MAP REF SX9255

The least commercialised part of Torbay, Brixham is home to a pretty harbour surrounded by some fine old buildings and a handful of pretty colour-washed cottages. Here the fish and chip shops, inexpensive cafés and other typical seaside outlets seem to try to blend in with their surroundings.

This is very much a seafaring community, as evidenced by the replica of Francis Drake's ship the *Golden Hind* in the harbour (open to the public) and the aquarium and trawling exhibition on the dockside. Fishing continues today but only on a small scale. The Brixham Museum on New Road traces the ebb and flow of the town's maritime fortunes over nine centuries of seafaring; you can get right up to date by visiting the working marina next to the harbour.

There are some fine beaches nearby – St Mary's Bay is large and sandy, but the rest are small shingle or pebble shores and are relatively peaceful and

■ Insight

CLOTTED CREAM

One of the most popular West Country experiences is to sample a clotted cream tea, and invitations to do so are found along most streets and country lanes. The delicious main ingredient, the clotted cream, is produced from milk with the highest cream content. It is left to stand in a pan for between 12 and 24 hours, then gently heated (never boiled) until a solid ring of clotted cream has formed around the edge. The pan is then left covered in a cool place for another 24 hours before the cream is skimmed from the top with a slotted spoon. Real Devon cream teas substitute Devonshire Splits, a kind of sweet bread roll, for the usual scones.

undeveloped. Just to the east of the town lies Berry Head Country Park, a splendid nature reserve, ideal for walking and for enjoying the views from the headland. The remains of a huge Napoleonic fort can also be visited here.

BURGH ISLAND MAP REF SX6544

One of the many curiosities of Devon, Burgh Island is a tiny rock covering just 28 acres (11ha). From the headland at Bigbury-on-Sea you can see all its points of interest. The largest structure, the rather unprepossessing box-shaped building is, surprisingly, a luxury hotel. Just to the right is the much humbler but atmospheric Pilchard Inn. Until the mid-19th century Burgh Island was a prosperous pilchard-fishing community and the 14th-century inn was simply a fisherman's cottage. High above it stands the Huer's Hut. A lookout was stationed here and when the great shoals of pilchards were spotted he would raise a hue and cry – hence the name.

Burgh Island is in fact only an island at high tide. At other times you can walk or drive – 'England 282 metres', says the sign! The most novel way to arrive, however, is at high tide, aboard the extraordinary Burgh Island sea tractor, which, with its passenger compartment raised high above the waves, can safely cross in up to 7 feet (2m) of water.

DARTINGTON MAP REF SX7862

The Dartington Estate was founded in 1925 when Leonard and Dorothy Elmhirst bought 14th-century Dartington Hall and gardens (the largest medieval house in the west of England) as part of

BURGH ISLAND HOTEL

The eccentric millionaire Archibald Nettlefold built Burgh Island Hotel in 1929. He owned the island and used the hotel as a guest house for his friends, who included the Duke of Windsor and Mrs Simpson, Noël Coward and Agatha Christie, who wrote here prolifically (*Evil Under the Sun* is set on the island). More recently Kirk Douglas and the Beatles have hidden themselves here. If you want to admire the hotel's art deco interior you'll need to book a room, or have Sunday lunch or a black-tie dinner.

a project to regenerate rural life in this part of Devon. The house, now brilliantly renovated, is part of a conference and arts centre that promotes one of the best programmes of music, theatre, films and arts courses in the Southwest. When not in use the spectacular Great Hall can be visited and the beautiful 25-acre (10ha) gardens are open daily.

The Dartington name has been made world-famous by the project's glittering success, the Dartington Crystal glass factory at Great Torrington. Opened in 1967, it now employs many skilled local craftspeople to create designs from top British designers.

The neighbouring Dartington Cider Press Centre is the finest small-scale shopping centre and, indeed, exhibition showcase in the region, with quality contemporary crafts, farm foods, plants, books, kitchenware, Dartington Glass and much more, drawing from both within and beyond the estate. The centre has a lovely setting around an old cider press with craft demonstrations.

DARTMOUTH   MAP REF SX8751

The ancient town and deep-water port of Dartmouth enjoys an unrivalled setting at the mouth of the picturesque River Dart, with steep green hills to either side and a busy, colourful estuary. The Embankment is a lovely uncluttered promenade, free of tourist trappings, and the attractive houses of Kingswear, many built for Dartmouth's wealthy merchants and sea captains, dot the far bank. Neither major road nor railway link has ever reached Dartmouth and this has undoubtedly helped the centre of town – a tiny web of criss-crossing cobbled streets and narrow alleyways – to retain its ancient atmosphere and to protect it from the onslaught of modern traffic that blights many coastal towns.

In the very centre is the Boatfloat, a charming inner harbour only accessible to small craft. In the tourist information office, on the corner of the car park, is Thomas Newcomen's Atmospheric Steam Engine, a 'nodding donkey' type of engine, invented in 1712, which is claimed to be the first ever successful steam engine. Also just off the Boatfloat, on Duke Street, is the 17th-century Butterwalk, a four-storey arcaded house decorated with wood carvings, its three upper floors supported by eleven granite pillars. It now houses shops and the delightful small Dartmouth Museum, with a whole flotilla of model ships and original 17th-century plaster and panelling. Further along Duke Street is the old cobbled market square and building, erected in 1829, now home to various permanent shops but still the site of the weekly market.

Two buildings that have survived from the 14th century are the Cherub pub, Dartmouth's oldest building (1380) and Agincourt House. The prettiest part of town, however, is the charming cobbled quayside of Bayard's Cove. The Pilgrim Fathers put into this cove in 1620 en route to the New World and around five centuries earlier the Crusaders departed from here. You can explore the shell of a fortress, which was built in 1510 to protect the entrance to the harbour.

Near the mouth of the river is Dartmouth Castle (English Heritage), a small fortification built in 1481 to stop sea raids on the town. It was added to in the 16th and 18th centuries and was the first to be designed specifically with gunports in mind, thus giving its cannons maximum angle of fire. The views from here are superb and as the castle was never harmed, it still retains its ancient atmosphere.

■ Visit

MARITIME TRADITIONS

Dartmouth has been an important port since early medieval times, when the Normans started trading regularly with their homeland. Richard the Lionheart and the Crusaders departed from here, while during the Middle Ages Dartmouth enjoyed considerable trade with Europe. By the 17th century, however, Bristol and London had become the major trade centres and Dartmouth retained only its naval duties. The famous Royal Britannia Naval College, high above the river, has trained the seafaring elite since 1905, including members of the present royal family. There are guided tours of the college during the summer.

DAWLISH   MAP REF SX9576

This pleasantly old-fashioned seaside resort, once the haunt of Charles Dickens and Jane Austen, is famous for its landscaped gardens, known as the Lawn. These stretch back from the front, flanked by two peaceful streams which are home to black swans. Around here you'll find some fine Regency, Georgian and Victorian buildings, and there is a small local museum on Barton Terrace. One curious feature is that the mainline train runs right alongside the beach. As many old local pictures confirm, this was a stirring sight in the days of steam and for most people it was the only way to get to the seaside.

To the north is Dawlish Warren and a 1.5-mile-long (2.4km) dune system that incorporates a large nature reserve. There is a pleasant coastal walk to the Warren from central Dawlish.

KINGSBRIDGE   MAP REF SX7344

Despite its modest size Kingsbridge has been known as 'the capital of the South Hams' since the 13th century, when it was granted its market charter, and ever since has been the regional market centre. Steep Fore Street, lined with speciality shops, rises up from the Quay, where there is a splendid leisure centre. This is the very highest point of the picturesque Kingsbridge estuary, the flooded river valley on which Salcombe also lies, and an enjoyable boat trip links the two towns in summer.

For many visitors the highlight of Kingsbridge is the excellent Cookworthy Museum of Rural Life in South Devon, in Fore Street. This is dedicated to William Cookworthy, a Quaker born in the town in 1705 and a pioneer in the English porcelain industry. The collection, set in a 17th-century schoolhouse, is one of the best of its kind in the region. It reflects many aspects of Devon life throughout the centuries and includes examples of a Victorian kitchen and an Edwardian pharmacy, plus a large farm gallery in a walled garden.

Towards the top of Fore Street is a colonnaded 16th-century street of shops, a 15th-century church and the town hall, with its odd-shaped 19th-century clock tower. Explore, too, the picturesque back streets and passages.

■ Visit

DAWLISH WARREN NATURE RESERVE

More than 450 plant species are protected at this 500-acre (200ha) nature reserve, including a number of orchids and the famous Warren crocus, only found here. A large hide looks out over the estuary, where sanderling, oystercatchers and terns can be seen. In mid winter the estuary is host to Brent geese and a flock of wintering avocets. There is a visitor centre where guided walks start from.

NEWTON ABBOT

MAP REF SX8571

Newton Abbot has been a market and crossroads town for centuries: first in medieval times, as it is on the main road between the major ports of Dartmouth and Exeter; later when granite from Haytor was shipped to London; then most importantly in 1846, when the railway arrived in town. Newton Abbot became the centre of the Great Western

Railway locomotive works, employing more than 600 people. The town's other claim to fame is its National Hunt horse-racing course and this, with other local history, is covered in the Newton Abbot Museum on St Paul's Road.

The most fascinating attraction in the town is Tucker's Maltings. This is Britain's only working malthouse open to the public (it produces enough malt to make 15 million pints of beer a year) and a lively guided tour covers the entire process of malting. You'll remember the evocative smells for a long time and adults can sample a glass of beer from the brewery that shares the premises.

Southwest of the town, off the A381 Totnes road, is Bradley Manor (National Trust), a small 11th-century manor house set in woodlands and meadows.

PAIGNTON MAP REF SX8860

Around a century ago Paignton was described as 'a neat and improving village and bathing place'. It remains a popular bathing place but is no longer a village, and, due to its amusement arcades, inexpensive cafés and discount stores, is often regarded as a poor relation to neighbouring Torquay. Paignton, however, is unabashed, and performs its role of provider of cheap holidays very effectively.

The beaches, some of the best in the Southwest, are the main draw, particularly Goodrington Sands, which has the region's largest water park. In summer it can be unbearably crowded, but there are other beaches of varying character in the vicinity. Although the town itself may appear devoid of high

■ **Visit**

ST JOHN'S CHURCH

Paignton's St John's Church, which dates from the 15th century, is an unusual blend of red sandstone and white Beer stone. The headless angels inside were damaged by the Puritans in the 17th century and there is also a grisly skeleton.

■ **Insight**

A ROYAL DECLARATION

At the centre of Newton Abbot is the ancient tower of St Leonard's, all that remains of the medieval church. Beside here a plaque marks the spot where the first declaration of William III, Prince of Orange, was read as he made his way from Brixham to London to assume the English throne. He stayed overnight in Forde House to the southeast of the town.

culture, there are historic houses to visit. Oldway Mansion, built by Isaac Singer (founder of the sewing-machine empire) in 1874, is now used as council offices, but the best rooms are open to the public. Just outside town, near Marldon, is Compton Castle (National Trust), a fortified manor house built between 1340 and 1520 and home to the descendants of Sir Humphrey Gilbert, who colonised Newfoundland. Paignton Zoo, in 75 acres (30ha) 1 mile (1.6km) from the town, is one of the largest zoos in the country, with all the favourites – lions, tigers, elephants, rhinos, monkeys and giraffes. For many visitors the finest thing to come out of Paignton is the Paignton and Dartmouth Steam Railway, which steams along a scenic line to Kingswear by the Dart estuary.

Bigbury-on-Sea and Burgh Island

This short walk, initially inland through farmland, returns to Bigbury-on-Sea via the dramatic coastal path. Just off Bigbury beach, 307yds (280m) from shore, lies craggy Burgh Island, which can still be reached by giant sea tractor whenever the tide is in. When the tide is out, however, you can simply stroll across the sand. Burgh Island Hotel became a fashionable venue for the jetset in the 1930s – Noël Coward and Agatha Christie were just some of its famous visitors.

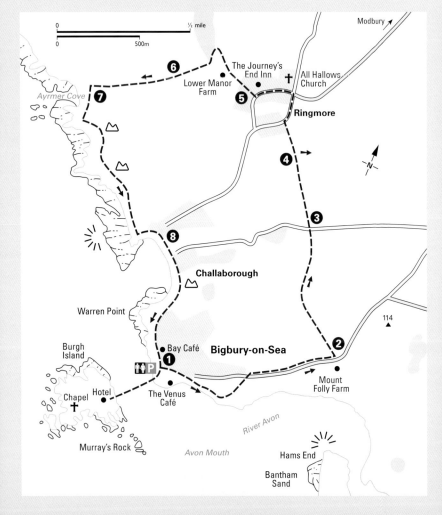

Route Directions

1 Leave the car park through the entrance. Follow coast path signs right (low tide route along beach to the seasonal ferry to Bantham, then left towards the road and right on to cliffs. Turn left before bungalows, then left to the road. Cross over, go through a kissing gate and turn right uphill, passing through two big gates, to reach a path junction near Mount Folly Farm.

2 Turn left along a gritty track (signed 'Ringmore'). At the field top is a path junction; go through the kissing gate and keep ahead downhill, signed 'Ringmore', with a fence right. Pass through a metal gate, drop through a kissing gate, keep ahead to another on a farm track; walk up the next field, crossing a stile on to a lane.

3 Cross over, following the signs for Ringmore, through a metal gate. Walk down into the next combe, keeping the hedgebank right. Cross the stream at the bottom on a concrete walkway, and go over a stile. Ignore the path left, but go straight ahead, uphill, through a plantation and enter a gate on to a narrow path between a fence and hedge.

4 Pass through a kissing gate, bear right then turn immediately left uphill to a path junction; pass through the kissing gate and follow the path to Ringmore. Turn right at the lane, then left at the church to find The Journey's End Inn on the right.

5 From the pub turn right down the narrow lane which gives way to a footpath. It winds round gardens to meet a tarmac lane. Turn left downhill. Walk straight on down the track, eventually passing Lower Manor Farm, and keep going down past the 'National Trust Ayrmer Cove' notice. After a small gate and stream crossing keep straight on at a path junction.

6 Pass through a kissing gate and walk towards the cove on a grassy path above the combe (left). Pass through gates and over a stile to gain the beach.

7 Follow coast path signs ('Challaborough') left over a small footbridge then climb very steeply uphill to the cliff top and great views over Burgh Island. The cliffs are unstable here – take care. The path leads to Challaborough – basically one huge holiday park.

8 Turn right along the beach road and pick up the track uphill along the coast towards Bigbury-on-Sea. Go straight on to meet the tarmac road, then bear right on the coast path to the car park.

Route facts

DISTANCE/TIME 4 miles (6.4km) 1h45

MAP OS Explorer OL20 South Devon

START Huge car park at Bigbury-on-Sea, grid ref: SX 652442

TRACKS Fields, tracks (muddy in winter), coast path, 3 stiles

GETTING TO THE START
Bigbury-on-Sea is signposted off the A379 between Plymouth and Kingsbridge. A mile (1.6km) east of Modbury, turn right on the B3392 towards Bigbury and Bigbury-on-Sea. On entering Bigbury-on-Sea there is a large pay-and-display car park by the beach on the left.

THE PUB The Pilchard Inn, Burgh Island.
Tel: 01548 810514;
www.burghisland.com

❶ Steep sections of narrow coast path close to the cliff edge.

SALCOMBE MAP REF SX7439

The great blue saucer of Salcombe Bay, aflutter with white triangular sails, surrounded by the green hills of the South Hams and fringed by golden pocket-handkerchief beaches, is one of south Devon's finest sights. Salcombe is among the largest yachting centres in England and several old wharf houses are workshops for boat makers and marine engineers.

The tiny golden beach of North Sands is adjacent to the picturesque ruin of Salcombe Castle/Fort Charles, which was built in 1544 as protection against French and Spanish raiders but was destroyed during the Civil War. Continue on to South Sands and Splat Cove or alternatively catch a ferry to one of the beaches on the other side of the bay.

About 1.5 miles (2.4km) southwest of Salcombe, at Sharpitor, is Overbecks Museum and Garden (National Trust), a charming Edwardian house largely dedicated to local maritime affairs. Overbecks' beautiful 6-acre (2.4ha) garden, set high above the estuary, is full of rare and exotic specimens which flourish in the area's mild micro-climate and is worth a visit for its views alone.

SLAPTON MAP REF SX8245

Slapton Sands is an uncommercialised 2-mile (3.2km) long windswept shingle ridge, a favourite spot for walking. Slapton Ley, which is divided from the beach by the road, is a freshwater lake, famous for its wildfowl. This is a National Nature Reserve and a public hide, for birding, is situated in the Torcross car park.

The village of Slapton (0.5 mile/800m inland and not to be confused with Torcross, at the southernmost part of Slapton Sands) features a fine medieval church. The impressive tower to the north of the church is all that remains of the College of Chantry Priests, founded in 1373. Just north of Slapton Sands is the unspoiled sandy cove of Blackpool Sands, rated by many as the best beach in the South Hams.

START POINT MAP REF SX8337

The dramatic southwesterly tip of the South Hams, Start Point has cliffs rising over 100 feet (30.5m) high. On the south side they are almost sheer and streaked by quartz veins which run through the dark rock. A lighthouse (tours available) warns shipping off the dangerous bank known as the Skerries. In Elizabethan times pirates were hung in chains here as a warning to other lawless seafarers.

From Start Point the coast path heads west along to Prawle Point, the most southern extremity of Devon. The latter, which can be lashed by the full fury of

■ **Visit**

D-DAY TRAINING

As part of the preparations for the D-Day landings in 1944, American troops used Slapton Sands for manoeuvres because of their similarity to the Normandy beaches. Tragically, while training, a convoy was attacked by German torpedo boats with the loss of nearly 1,000 lives. An American Sherman tank in the car park at Torcross is a memorial to this event. The tank was lost from a landing craft during the attack but was remarkably salvaged from 65 feet (20m) of water in 1984.

the waves in stormy weather, has been chiselled and chipped into an almost vertical drop beneath the coastguard lookout station.

TEIGNMOUTH MAP REF SX9473

The bright red cliffs with a verdant fringe and the red sand beaches of Teignmouth (pronounced Tin-muth) make this a distinctive seafront, complete with an old-fashioned pier.

The town became a fashionable holiday resort in the late 18th and early 19th centuries and if you look along Powderham Terrace or the Den, or just up above the fronts of the many cafés and tourist shops, you will see that it retains a good deal of its Georgian and early Victorian architecture. The Quays are full of character; this is the old harbour area, which has for centuries shipped huge quantities of Bovey ball clay and Dartmoor granite. A small fishing fleet also operates from here. You can learn more about the town's local and maritime history in the museum in French Street.

A narrow bridge connects Teignmouth to pretty Shaldon village. There the houses, many of which date back to Georgian times, are packed so closely together that the only sensible way of visiting the village is by ferry from Teignmouth, a service that dates back to Elizabethan times.

There's a fine church to see but the favourite attraction is the charming Shaldon Wildlife Trust. It is a breeding centre for rare and endangered species of small mammals, exotic birds and reptiles and because of its tiny size many

■ Visit

DISAPPEARING HALLSANDS

The village of Hallsands, northwest of Start Point, was once a prosperous fishing community of 37 houses. In the early years of the 20th century its protective offshore shingle bank was dredged to provide materials for building dockyards in Plymouth. As a result of this the beach level dropped and in 1917 storms destroyed all but one of the houses. Today Hallsands is a popular and picturesque shingle sunbathing beach (swimming can be dangerous) and traces of the lost village can be seen a couple of minutes' walk beyond the block of luxury holiday apartments, formerly a hotel.

of its inmates are very tame. Close by, the erroneously named 'Smuggler's tunnel' leads down to Shaldon's own beach, the Ness, backed by a bold red cliff. From the top of here there are some marvellous views of Teignmouth and the Teign estuary.

TORQUAY MAP REF SX9164

Torquay is the south Devon at its most continental – a balmy climate, palm trees sparkling with coloured lights and millionaires' yachts basking in the marina. The large number of English language students and foreign tourists adds an exotic chatter to the town. Yet this is also the capital of the English Riviera – the birthplace of Agatha Christie and more famously the fictional setting of the classic BBC TV series *Fawlty Towers*. Don't expect to find the actual hotel here, however, as the series was filmed elsewhere.

From humble beginnings as a fishing village, the town's resort career began during Napoleonic times, and during the height of the Victorian era its mild winters were attracting consumptives and fashionable visitors on doctors' orders. By 1850 it was proclaiming itself 'Queen of the Watering Holes' and today it is still one of the most popular seaside resorts in the country.

The centre of town is the lively marina and harbour, including the listed copper-domed Edwardian Pavilion, which now houses an excellent shopping centre. Eastwards the cliffs rise up to Daddy Hole Plain, a great chasm in the cliff where the plain meets the sea, and the views from here are superb. Continue east to the point at Hope's Nose for more sea panoramas.

The beaches, though not as broad and sandy as those to be found at neighbouring Paignton, are numerous and spread well apart, which helps to dissipate the summer crowds. The most attractive of the major beaches is Oddicombe, with its picturesque backdrop of steep sandstone cliffs topped by lush woodland. The descent is steep and a cliff railway runs down 720 feet (220m) to the shingle below.

The Oddicombe/Babbacombe area is also home to Torquay's best tourist attractions. Kents Caverns form one of the most important prehistoric sites in Europe, where a fascinating and atmospheric half a mile (800m) guided tour takes you back through two million years of history, with many natural spectacular rock formations. More cave finds can be seen at the Torquay Museum on Babbacombe Road. The museum has a wide range of galleries and some fascinating displays.

Another excellent wet-weather option, in the charming St Marychurch parish, is Bygones, a life-size re-creation of a Victorian street, illustrating shops and dwellings, including an ironmonger, grocer, sweet shop and apothecary, with minute nostalgic details right down to authentic smells. Visit the giant model railway and the walk-through Trench Experience with the sights, sounds and smells of the First World War.

One of Torquay's favourite attractions is Babbacombe Model Village, a really outstanding piece of design, full of interest for all ages, and regarded as a masterpiece of miniature landscape gardening. A nice sense of typically English humour pervades the village, with the minuscule Lord Elpusall waiting to show you his one-twelfth size stately home. Visit again by night (Easter and summer only), to see the miniature illuminations; on wet days enjoy the 4-D theatre experiences.

Next to the harbour is Torre Abbey, from where the town derives its name. Originally constructed in the 12th century, the abbey was dissolved and subsumed into a 16th-century mansion, itself remodelled in the Georgian period. It now holds the municipal art gallery, featuring works of art by 19th-century artists and a local history collection. In the grounds are monastic ruins, the well-preserved abbey gatehouse, exotic gardens and a splendid 12th-century tithe barn, known as the Spanish Barn, since it was used in 1588 to hold around

400 Armada prisoners who had been captured by Sir Francis Drake.

Just a mile (1.6km) west from the centre of town is the picture-postcard village of Cockington, a crossroads gathering of thatched cottages with an old smithy, the village stocks, a mill pond and working waterwheel. Despite the number of summer visitors and the inevitable tea shops that have sprung up, this is still a beautiful and largely unspoiled place. The grounds and gardens of 19th-century Cockington Court are open to the public and include a café, craft centre and gallery.

TOTNES MAP REF SX8060

This ancient picturesque town set high on a hill above the River Dart is one of south Devon's gems. Its well preserved Norman and Tudor features make it one of the West Country's most attractive towns. A Norman castle, a 15th-century church tower and the 16th-century High Street are some of its main attractions.

■ Insight

AGATHA CHRISTIE

One of Britain's best-loved and most successful authors, Agatha Christie was born at Barton in Torquay and frequently returned to the county of her birth. Her books have been translated into more than a hundred languages and there have been countless film and TV adaptations, but she maintained her own air of mystery and little is known about her private life.
A huge selection of Agatha Christie-related products – books, DVDs, souvenirs – can be found at the tourist information office; the Agatha Christie Festival takes place every September.

At the bottom of the town the Steamer Quay, once a thriving river port, is still home to many working boats, while pleasure trips also run from here to Dartmouth. Another way of arriving (or leaving) is via the South Devon Railway steam train from Buckfastleigh along the beautiful Dart Valley.

From the quay steep, claustrophobic Fore Street climbs into the centre of Totnes, passing several fine 16th- and 17th-century merchants' houses. Their wealth was established in medieval and Tudor times when the export of wool and tin from Dartmoor made Totnes one of England's richest towns.

One of the finest buildings is the Elizabethan House, beautifully restored to house the lively local museum. Partly timbered and dating back to 1575, it features furniture, domestic objects, toys, dolls, railway paraphernalia and a Victorian grocer's shop. One room of the house is dedicated to Charles Babbage, the pioneering computer scientist and mathematician, who originated the concept of a programmable computer.

Continue up the hill and it becomes apparent why Totnes has declared itself to be the 'health-food capital of the West Country', with a plethora of wholefood shops and eating places. But if you turn right just past the handsome Tudor East Gate Arch, into the charming Ramparts Walk, you will come to the Guildhall, a preserved 16th-century building where you can see the old jail and a table where Oliver Cromwell sat in 1646. Perhaps most remarkable of all is the fact that the present town council still meets here.

Back on Fore Street seek out the pillared shop arcades, or shambles, of the Butterwalk and Poultry Walk, which once sheltered the markets which were held here. A lively local market is held opposite the Butterwalk every Friday and Saturday, while on Tuesdays in summer the town plays host to a costumed Elizabethan charity market.

There are more costumes to be seen inside the Butterwalk at the Devonshire Collection of Period Costume, housed in the superbly renovated Bogan House, built around 1500.

At the top of the hill is Totnes Castle (English Heritage). This perfect example of a small Norman motte-and-bailey fortress, has wonderful views over the town and the River Dart. On Coronation Road you will find Totnes Town Mill, which houses the tourist information centre, a restored Victorian waterwheel and mill machinery, and an excellent interpretative exhibition showing the development of Totnes.

YEALMPTON MAP REF SX5851

Yealmpton, pronounced Yampton, is a small village on the edge of the South Hams between Modbury and Plymouth. The parish church of St Bartholomew is well worth exploring for a number of reasons. In the churchyard is a Roman pillar, the font is Saxon, while highly polished marble from Kitley Quarries (part of the Kitley House Estate) features in the walls, chancel screen and altar table. St Bartholomew's was rebuilt in 1850 and Sir John Betjeman referred to it as the 'most amazing' Victorian church in the county.

■ Visit

PREHISTORIC RESIDENTS

As far as we know, the earliest human occupation of these islands was around 400,000 years ago and Kents Cavern is one of only two sites in the country that provide evidence to this effect (the other is a modern quarry in Somerset). At Torquay a layer of conglomerate limestone revealed simple tools and signs of stone working from that date, as well as the earlier remains of animals such as sabre-toothed tigers, mammoths and bears.

■ Visit

A FLAVOUR OF HISTORIC SHALDON

Every Wednesday in summer Shaldon turns the clock back to 1785 with traders dressed in period costume, special craft stalls and evening entertainment.

■ Visit

TWO ANCIENT WATERING HOLES

Walk to the top of Fore Street in Totnes and then on up into the Narrows – the reason for the name is obvious – then turn left into Leechwell Street and you will come to the town's oldest pub, the picturesque 17th-century Kingsbridge Inn. To the left a narrow passage, Leechwell Lane, runs down to an ancient well with three granite troughs. This was once thought to have had medicinal properties.

■ Insight

OLD MOTHER HUBBARD

Yealmpton is the home of Old Mother Hubbard, so to speak. The famous rhyme was written locally in 1805 and the lady in question is thought to have been a housekeeper at Kitley House. Old Mother Hubbard's Cottage, to which she retired in the late 1700s, is a perfect 16th-century Devon cob and thatch building at the east end of the village.

East Portlemouth to Limebury Point

Follow this coastal stroll from the hamlet of East Portlemouth, which has some of the best views in the area. From Limebury Point you can see across the estuary to Overbecks (National Trust), an elegant Edwardian house in a magnificent setting above South Sands. A ferry connects East Portlemouth and Salcombe.

Route Directions

1 Park on the verge near the phone box at East Portlemouth (or in the parking area – village hall fund contributions). Go across the parking area and steeply downhill on a narrow tarmac footpath signposted 'Salcombe', which gives way to steep steps.

2 When you reach the lane at the bottom of the steps, turn right if you want to visit The Venus Café and catch the ferry to Salcombe. If

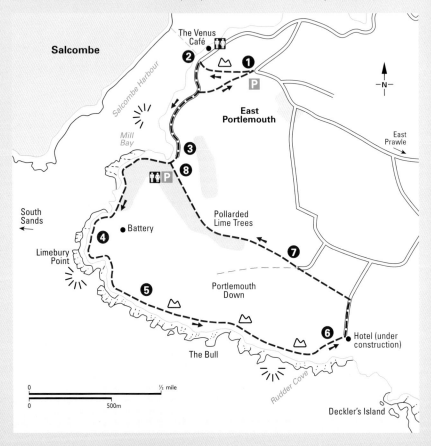

you want to get on with the walk, turn left along the lane as it follows the edge of the estuary. This is the official route of the coast path and it passes beside some very exclusive residences.

3 The lane leads to the pretty, sandy beach at Mill Bay. Carefully follow the acorn coast path signs for Gara Rock through a sycamore wood, with lovely views across the estuary, and glimpses of inviting little coves.

4 At Limebury Point you reach open cliff, from where there are great views to South Sands and Overbecks opposite and craggy Bolt Head. The coast path now bears eastwards below Portlemouth Down, which was divided into strip fields in the late 19th century.

5 The path along this stretch undulates steeply, and is rocky in places. Keep going until you reach the bench and viewpoint over the beach at Rickham Sands. Just beyond this, as the coast path continues right (there is reasonable access to the beach), take the left fork and climb steeply up below the lookout to reach a signpost by the site of the old Gara Rock Hotel (demolished in 2006).

6 Turn left to reach the former hotel drive (now apartments) and walk straight on up the lane. After 250yds (229m) turn left through a gate in the hedge signposted 'Mill Bay'. Walk straight ahead through a gate and across the field, bearing right to a gate; note Malborough church in the distance. Go through a small copse, then a gate and across the farm track. Go through a gate down the public bridleway.

7 This runs gradually downhill beneath huge, ancient, pollarded lime trees, with a grassy combe to the right. The path leads past the car park to reach Mill Bay.

8 Turn right along the lane. If you want to avoid the steps, look out for a footpath sign pointing right, up a narrow, steep, path to regain East Portlemouth and your car; if not, continue along the lane and retrace your route up the steps.

Route facts

DISTANCE/TIME 4 miles (6.4km) 2h

MAP OS Explorer OL20 South Devon

START Near phone box in East Portlemouth or in small parking bay, grid ref: SX 746386

TRACKS Good coast path, field paths and tracks, no stiles

GETTING TO THE START East Portlemouth is about 9 miles (14.5km) southeast of Kingsbridge on narrow and winding roads. From Kingsbridge take the A379 towards Dartmouth. After 4 miles (6.4km), turn right at Frogmore, following signs for East Portlemouth for 5 miles (8km). Park on the roadside next to the phone box, opposite cottages. Or park in the village car park straight ahead.

THE PUB The Victoria Inn, Salcombe. Tel 01548 842604; www.victoriainnsalcombe.co.uk

❶ Undulating terrain, sometimes steep and rocky, coastal path

What to look for

Many stretches of the coast path are resplendent with wild flowers virtually all year, and during the summer the path below Portlemouth Down is incredible. There are banks of purple wild thyme, heather, gorse, red campion, bladder campion, tiny yellow tormentil and pretty blue scabious. Look too for the common dodder, a parasitic plant with pretty clusters of pink flowers.

Along Cliffs to Dartmouth Castle

An easy round walk along the cliffs to Blackstone Point and Dartmouth Castle – and a ferry ride to the pub. The 15th-century Dartmouth Castle was built to protect the homes and warehouses of the town's merchants.

Route Directions

1 Go through the right-hand National Trust car park, following the signs 'Coast Path Dartmouth'. Continue through a kissing gate, keeping the hedge to your right. Walk through the next field, then through a gate and another kissing gate to join the coast path.

2 Turn left; there are lovely views west to Start Point and east towards the Day Beacon above Kingswear. The coast path runs a little inland from

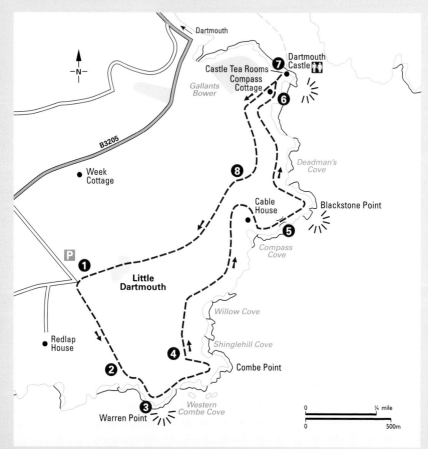

the cliff edge, but you can walk out on to Warren Point (a plaque reveals that the Devon Federation of Women's Institutes gave this land to the National Trust in 1970).

3 From Warren Point follow the coast to pass above Western Combe Cove (with steps down to the sea) and then Combe Point (take care – it's a long drop to the sea from here).

4 Rejoin the coast path through an open gateway in a wall and follow it above Shinglehill Cove. The path turns inland, passes a pond and follows a track, then bears right along the back of Willow Cove. It passes above woods (with a field left) and then climbs to pass through a gate. Follow the yellow arrow ahead to reach a footpath post, then turn sharp right down the valley, bearing right at the bottom to a stile as signed. Follow the path on, and through a gate near Compass Cove.

5 Follow the coast path left over a footbridge, and continue walking towards Blackstone Point. The path turns inland to run along the side of the estuary through deciduous woodland.

6 The path meets a surfaced lane opposite Compass Cottage; keep ahead on to the lane and immediately right again steeply downhill. Follow coast path signs right to zig-zag steeply down then up steps to reach a turning space, then go right down steps to reach the castle and café.

7 Retrace your route up the steps, then turn left up the lane to Point 6, then left to pass Compass Cottage, and continue straight on up the steep lane (signposted 'Little Dartmouth') and through a kissing gate on to National Trust land.

8 The path runs along the top of a field and through a five-bar gate on to a green lane. Go through a gate and the farmyard at Little Dartmouth and ahead on a tarmac lane to the car park.

Route facts

DISTANCE/TIME 3.5 miles (5.7km) 2h

MAP OS Explorer OL20 South Devon

START National Trust car park at Little Dartmouth, grid ref: SX 874491

TRACKS Easy coastal footpath, green lanes, 1 stile

GETTING TO THE START Little Dartmouth is about 2 miles (3.2km) south of Dartmouth on the A379. Approaching Dartmouth on the A3122, turn right along the A379 towards Stoke Fleming. Turn left in 1 mile (1.6km), signposted to Little Dartmouth Farm, and keep ahead at the next crossroads, following signs for the farm. At the next junction turn left for the National Trust car park.

THE PUB The Royal Castle Hotel, Dartmouth. Tel 01803 833033; www.royalcastle.co.uk. Drive to Dartmouth or take the ferry from Stumpy Steps.

❶ Generally easy, but extra care needs to be taken if walking with children along the clifftop paths.

What to look for

Dartmouth, both on shore and on the water, is always buzzing with activity. There's lots to watch, including pleasure steamers, private cruisers, dinghies, rowing boats, ferries, expensive ocean-going yachts, canoeists and even huge cruise ships, calling in for a night on route for sunnier climes. You'll also notice naval craft.

■ TOURIST INFORMATION CENTRES

English Riviera Tourist Board
Vaughan Parade, Torquay.
Tel: 01803 296296;
www.englishriviera.co.uk
(for Brixham, Paignton and Torquay)

Dartmouth
The Engine House,
Mayor's Avenue.
Tel: 01803 834224;
www.discoverdartmouth.com

Dawlish
The Lawn. Tel: 01626 215665;
www.visitsouthdevon.co.uk

Kingsbridge
The Quay. Tel: 01548 853195;
www.kingsbridgeinfo.co.uk

Modbury
5 Modbury Court.
Tel: 01548 830159;
www.modburytic.org.uk

Newton Abbot
6 Bridge House, Courtenay
Street. Tel: 01626 215667;
www.visitsouthdevon.co.uk

Salcombe
Council Hall, Market Street.
Tel: 01548 843927;
www.salcombeinformation.
co.uk

Teignmouth
The Den, Sea Front.
Tel: 01626 215666;
www.visitsouthdevon.co.uk

Totnes
Town Mill, Coronation Road.
Tel: 01803 863168;
www.totnesinformation.co.uk

■ PLACES OF INTEREST

Babbacombe Model Village
Hampton Avenue,
Babbacombe.
Tel: 01803 315315; www.
babbacombemodelvillage.
co.uk

Berry Pomeroy Castle
Totnes. Tel: 01803 866618;
www.english-heritage.org.uk

Bradley Manor
Newton Abbot.
Tel: 01626 661907;
www.nationaltrust.org.uk

Britannia Royal Naval College
Dartmouth.
Tel: 01803 832141;
www.royalnavy.mod.uk

Brixham Museum
Brixham. Tel: 01803 856267;
www.brixhamheritage.org.uk

Cockington Country Park
Torquay. Tel: 01803 606035;
www.countryside-trust.org.uk

Compton Castle
Compton. Tel: 01803 661906;
www.nationaltrust.org.uk

Dartmouth Castle
Dartmouth.
Tel: 01803 833588;
www.english-heritage.org.uk

Dartmouth Museum
6 Butterwalk, Dartmouth.
Tel: 01803 832923;
www.devonmuseums.net

Guildhall
Rampart Walk, Totnes.
Tel: 01803 862147; www.
totnestowncouncil.gov.uk

Oldway Mansion
Torquay Road, Paignton.

Tel: 01803 207933;
www.torquay.com

Overbeck's Museum and Garden
Sharpitor. Tel: 01548 842893;
www.nationaltrust.org.uk

Paignton and Dartmouth Steam Railway
Torbay Road, Paignton.
Tel: 01803 555872; www.
paignton-steamrailway.co.uk

Paignton Zoo
Totnes Road, Paignton.
Tel: 01803 697500;
www.paigntonzoo.org.uk

Salcombe Maritime Museum
Market Street.
www.devonmuseums.net

Shaldon Wildlife Trust
Ness Drive, Shaldon.
Tel: 01626 872234; www.
shaldonwildlifetrust.org.uk

Start Point Lighthouse Tours
Tel: 01803 771802;
www.trinityhouse.co.uk

Torquay Museum
529 Babbacombe Road,
Torquay. Tel: 01803 293975;
www.torquaymuseum.org

Torre Abbey Historic House and Gallery
The Kings Drive, Torquay.
Tel: 01803 293593;
www.torre-abbey.org.uk

Totnes Castle
Totnes. Tel: 01803 864406;
www.english-heritage.org.uk

Tuckers Maltings
Teign Road, Newton Abbot.
Tel: 01626 334734;
www.tuckersmaltings.co.uk

■ FOR CHILDREN

Prickly Ball Farm and Hedgehog Hospital
Denbury Road, near Newton Abbot. Tel: 01626 362319; www.pricklyballfarm.com

Quaywest Waterpark
Paignton. Tel: 01803 555550; www.splashdownquaywest.co.uk

Totnes Rare Breeds Farm
Littlehampton.
Tel: 01803 840387; www.totnesrarebreeds.co.uk

Woodlands Leisure Park
Blackawton, near Dartmouth.
Tel: 01803 712598

■ SHOPPING

Brixham
Pannier Market, Mon, Tue and Wed.

Dartmouth
Farmers' market, 2nd Sat.

Dawlish Warren
Produce market, 1st Fri.

Kingsbridge
Farmers' market, 1st and 3rd Sat.

Newton Abbot
Farmers' market, Tue.

Torquay
Farmers' Market, Fri.

Totnes
Elizabethan Market, May–Sep, Tue.
Market Civic Hall, Fri and Sat.

LOCAL SPECIALITIES
Dartington Cider Press Centre
Totnes.

Tel: 01803 847500; www.dartington.org

■ PERFORMING ARTS

Babbacombe Theatre
Torquay. Tel: 01803 328385; www.babbacombetheatre.com

Princess Theatre
Torbay Road, Torquay.
Tel: 08702 414120; www.englishriviera.co.uk

■ SPORTS & ACTIVITIES
BEACHES

Bigbury-on-Sea
Bigbury (Blue Flag).
Challaborough (Blue Flag).

Brixham
Breakwater Beach. Churston Cove. Fishcombe. Shoalstone. St Mary's Bay.

Dartmouth
Blackpool Sands (Blue Flag), Strete Gate. Slapton Sands. Torcross.

Dawlish
Boat Cove. Coryton Cove. Dawlish Warren (Blue Flag). Shell Cove.

Paignton
Broadsands Beach. Elberry Cove. Fairy Cove. Goodrington Sands. Paignton Sands. Preston Sands. Saltern Cove.

Salcombe
North Sands. Millbay, Sunny Cove. South Sands.

Teignmouth
Herring Cove. Mackerel Cove. Ness Cove. Teignmouth Beach.

Torquay
Ansteys Cove. Babbacombe. Corbyn Sands. Livermead. Maidencombe. Meadfoot Beach (Blue Flag). Oddicombe (Blue Flag). Preston Sands. Torre Abbey Sands.

BOAT TRIPS
Dartmouth
Riverlink, Lower Street.
Tel: 01803 835248; www.riverlink.co.uk
Dartmouth Boat Hire Centre, North Embankment.
Tel: 01803 834600; www.dartmouth-boat-hire.co.uk

CYCLE HIRE
Totnes
B R Trott, Warland Grange.
Tel: 01803 862493; www.brtrott.co.uk

HORSE-RIDING
Cockington
Cockington Riding Stables, Cockington Village.
Tel: 01803 606860

SAILING
Dartmouth
Dittisham Sailing School.
Tel: 01803 722365; www.discoverdartmouth.com

Teignmouth
Teign Corinthian Yacht Club, Dawlish Road.
Tel: 01626 772734; www.tcyc.org.uk

Torquay
Torbay Sea School, South Quay. Tel: 01803 665556; www.torbayseaschool.co.uk

SALCOMBE

Tea Rooms

Anne of Cleves
**56 Fore Street,
Totnes TQ9 5RU
Tel: 01803 863186**
The array of sumptuous gateaux in the window cannot fail to draw you into this cosy, old-fashioned tea shop. All the cakes are made on the premises – the layered chocolate fudge cake topped with chocolate curls and strawberries and the Bakewell tart decorated with cherries are both divine.

Avon Mill Café
**Avon Mill Garden Centre, Woodleigh Road, Loddiswell TQ7 4DD
Tel: 01548 550066;
www.avonmill.com**
This light and airy café with polished wood floors and local arts and crafts for sale is in a lovely old mill in the pretty wooded valley of the Avon river. It is a great place for a cream tea or light lunch. Don't miss the excellent deli selling local produce.

Hill House Tearoom
**Landscove, nr Ashburton TQ18 7LY. Tel: 01803 762261
www.hillhousenursery.com**
The perfect combination: a licensed tea room and a superb, old-fashioned plant nursery in the grounds of a beautiful country house by Landscove church. Delicious cream teas, home-made cakes and light lunches; seating inside or in the garden, listening to the rooks.

The Rocket House
**Torcross, Slapton Sands TQ7 2TQ. Tel: 01548 580697;
www.seabreezebreaks.com**
Overlooking Start Bay, this whitewashed, thatched cottage with bright blue shutters is a real find in this tucked-away corner of the South Hams. Food is home-made and locally sourced where possible. Enjoy cream teas, cakes, local ice cream and chunky sandwiches. Kite-surfing, bicycle hire and B&B are all available here too.

Pubs

Ferry Boat Inn
**Dittisham TQ6 0EX
Tel: 01803 722368**
The Ferry Boat Inn claims to have the 'best view from any pub window in the world'. The setting on the historic quayside overlooking the River Dart is certainly beautiful. The low-beamed bar is stuffed with nautical memorabilia and local fish is on the menu. Try local crab or Thai-style tuna fishcakes served with salad.

The Hope and Anchor
**Hope Cove, nr Salcombe TQ7 3HQ. Tel: 01548 561294;
www.hopeandanchor.co.uk**
A spacious yet characterful pub at Inner Hope, just opposite a small sandy beach and with fabulous views. The food is excellent, and portions generous: fish features strongly on the menu (lemon sole and Salcombe crab salad). Sit on the decking and watch the sunset.

Churston Court
**Churston, Brixham TQ5 0JE
Tel: 01803 842186;
www.churstoncourt.co.uk**
A visit to this huge Grade I listed inn is an extraordinary experience, as it used to be a Saxon manor and was once the haunt of sea captains and smugglers. Huge inglenook fireplaces, flagstone floors, weaponry (and the odd suit of armour) fill every room. On the menu is fresh fish.

The Tower Inn
**Slapton, nr Dartmouth TQ7 2PN. Tel: 01548 580216;
www.thetowerinn.com**
A mile from Slapton Sands, this inn was built as cottages to house the men working on the Collegiate Chantry of St Mary. Expect church-pew seating, a lovely garden and a sophisticated menu.

Exeter & East Devon

This quiet corner of Devon is a delight to explore because, although it is one of the most accessible from the rest of England, bisected by both the M5 and the A30, it has retained much of its old world character. Its countryside of rolling pastures and river valleys is dotted with unspoiled villages and even its resorts – Seaton, Sidmouth, Budleigh Salterton and Exmouth – preserve the quiet dignity of their Regency and Victorian heyday. Exeter, on the other hand, is an attractive and fascinating city, balancing its long and important history with the needs of its lively modern community.

9 Walk start point

BUDLEIGH SALTERTON

Unmissable attractions

The Jurassic Coast, the stretch of coastline between Exmouth and Studland Bay in Dorset, is a UNESCO World Heritage Site and is famous for its unspoiled cliffs and beautiful beaches. This coast also has some lovely towns and villages such as Branscombe and Beer. Inland, there are the attractions of Devon's main city, Exeter, with its vast cathedral, as well as Killerton House and Gardens further north, which has woodland walks in its 2,500-acre (1,012ha) estate. If you find yourself in this area near 5 November, then make sure you go and witness the incredible (and dangerous) sight of local men racing through the streets carrying burning barrels of tar at this centuries-old event in the otherwise tranquil village of Ottery St Mary.

1

1 **Beer**
This pretty seaside fishing village is part of the East Devon World Heritage Coast.

2 **Exeter Cathedral**
Magnificent Exeter Cathedral has a spectacular roof – the longest unbroken Gothic vault in the world.

3 **Exmouth**
This seaside town is known for its 2-mile (3.2km) golden sandy beach, and is a great place to go sailing.

AXMINSTER MAP REF SX2998

The name of this pleasant Devon town is inextricably linked with the world-famous carpets that are still produced here. The industry was begun in 1755 by Thomas Whitty, whose factory produced custom-made carpets of the highest quality for some of Britain's greatest mansions and palaces. Sadly, despite their popularity, factory tours have been stopped by safety regulations.

Apart from its carpets, Axminster is a busy market town with attractive streets set around the central Trinity Square (actually a triangle), which is dominated by the church. Nearby, the Old Court House in Church Street now serves as the town's information centre and just behind it is a lovely courtyard garden.

Just to the southwest of Axminster, tucked away in the country lanes south of the A35 Honiton road, is Shute Barton Manor (National Trust). This delightful old house with battlemented turrets dates from about 1380 and is one of the most important surviving non-fortified manor houses in the country. Shute Barton has been occupied by the Carew Pole family since the 16th century and their presence accounts for much of the houses's charm, with its family paraphernalia such as fishing rods, wellington boots and toys; the family dogs may well greet you in the hall.

AXMOUTH MAP REF SY2591

Axmouth is not only very pretty, it has been here a very long time. The Roman Fosse Way crossed the wide River Axe here, and by the 7th century the settlement was well established.

Today it presents a picturesque scene of colour-washed thatched cottages grouped around St Michael's Church, which dates back to Norman times. The village was once an important port, but as the river silted up, the size of vessels able to navigate it reduced until it could only accommodate yachts and pleasure craft. It is popular not only with weekend sailors, but also with windsurfers and birdwatchers, and a lovely walk alongside the estuary gives access to the Axmouth–Lyme Regis undercliffs.

BEER MAP REF SY2289

The lovely little fishing village of Beer occupies one of the most sheltered positions along this coast and its fishermen gained a reputation for hardy seamanship because they could put to sea when others were kept at home by the pounding waves. Beer is not only noted for its fishermen, it also has the most westerly chalk cliffs in England,

■ Insight

A SMUGGLER'S TALE

Jack Rattenbury, born in Beer in 1778, was Devon's most notorious smuggler. Having been disillusioned by the life of a fisherman, he went to sea as an honest crewman, but his vessel was captured by the French and various escapades took him back and forth across the Atlantic. After this, life in Beer was dull, and smuggling offered him the money and excitement he craved. There followed a life of forays across the Channel for contraband, dodging the Excise men, several prison sentences and some daring escapes. Nothing deterred him from his life of crime. His story was eventually recorded by a retired minister.

contrasting vividly with the deep red cliffs nearby and the lush green of the surrounding countryside. It was once home to a renowned lace-making industry, established here by refugees from the Netherlands, and the quality of the work rivalled the more famous Honiton lace.

Above Beer is Pecorama, set high on a hillside overlooking the village and the coastline. Apart from beautiful cultivated gardens, it also has a miniature steam and diesel passenger railway, which offers some of the best views across Lyme Bay, as well as an exhibition of railway modelling.

The Beer Quarry Caves offer a totally different experience, with an hour-long tour of these man-made caverns that extend for a quarter of a mile (400m) in each direction. The Romans worked these quarries nearly 2,000 years ago, and the vast caverns with vaulted roofs and natural stone pillars were hewn by hand over the intervening centuries. The Cretaceous limestone quarried at Beer was highly prized by stone masons. Soft and easy to carve when it first comes out of the ground, it hardens when it is exposed to the elements. Creamy-white in colour and smooth in texture, it provides a perfect medium for their craft, which can be seen to its best advantage in Exeter Cathedral.

BICTON PARK MAP REF SY0786

The beautiful gardens at Bicton were created in about 1730 to designs by the great André le Nôtre, the gardener to Louis XIV and the famed architect of the magnificent gardens at Versailles. If you stand in front of the orangery and look down over the three terraces of lawns, you will see formal flower beds and statues, with a great rectangular pond and its central fountain at the lowest level. From there the eye is drawn up again through a swathe cut between the trees to a distant obelisk. This is the focal point of the 50 acres (20ha) of Bicton Park, but there are many other delights to explore. Just to one side is the American Garden, establied in the 1830s, with rocky outcrops and some interesting trees from that continent. Here, too, is the Shell House, built of flints but containing shells from around the world. There are glasshouses too, including the Temperate House, Tropical House, Arid House and Palm House.

The Pinetum and Arboretum is home to a fine collection of more than 1,000 trees, representing 300 species, many of which are endangered in the wild. It also has 25 champion trees – the largest of their kind in the British Isles. At 41m (134ft) their champion Grecian fir is the tallest ever recorded.

One of the best introductions to the park can be gained from taking a ride on Bicton's narrow-gauge railway, which departs from a station near the entrance and hauls purpose-built carriages past the lake and through the Pinetum, taking in wonderful views of the Italian Gardens, before making a loop round to the Hermitage Garden.

Other attractions include an excellent countryside museum with wagons and a vintage cider press among its displays, an indoor soft-play area for younger children and an outdoor playground.

Broadhembury

This walk passes through the beech woods and farmland around Broadhembury.
The village's picturesque main street is lined with well-preserved cob and thatched
cottages and pretty flower-filled gardens, while the small, thatched Drewe Arms,
in the village centre, is an ideal place to stop for a drink and a bite to eat.

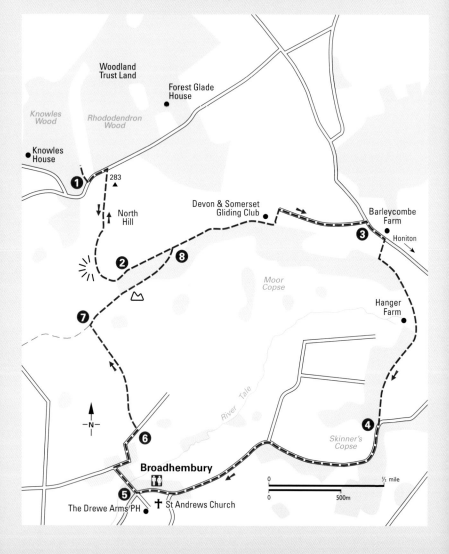

Route Directions

1 Return to the road and turn left uphill. Very shortly a bridleway sign points right, through another parking area. Follow this path – with wonderful views west – along the perimeter of the airfield, eventually ascending to a wooden gate.

2 Go though the gate and turn right along the edge of the airfield, eventually keeping to the right of the clubhouse. Follow the tarmac drive right, over a cattle grid, and keep ahead to join a road.

3 Turn right; pass Barleycombe Farm (on the left), then follow bridleway signs right, through a gate, downhill then left through another and into a field. Walk along the bottom of the field. The path curves right through a stand of beech trees and a metal gate, then runs straight across the next field towards a big beech tree and gate. Take the stony track through the gate. Keeping the fence on the right walk on to pass through a gate, with a coniferous plantation to the right.

4 The path ends at a lane; turn right downhill into Broadhembury. At St Andrew's Church cross the road and go through the churchyard (no dogs allowed), then under the lychgate and downhill to find The Drewe Arms (see left) for a welcome break.

5 To continue the walk, from the pub, turn left down the main street to reach the bridge and ford. Turn right up the lane, past the playground and up the hill, eventually bearing right.

6 Just past two thatched cottages (on the right) go left over the stile in the hedge and up the field, aiming for a stile in the top left corner. Go over that and straight ahead, passing to the left of the farmhouse and barn conversions. Over the next stile; round the next, then cross another; then right, round the edge of the field, and over two small stiles into a small copse. Another stile leads into the next field; bear slightly right to locate the next stile in the beech hedge opposite, which takes you into a green lane.

7 Turn right and walk uphill with conifers left and fields right until a metal gate leads to another and back on to the airfield.

Route facts

DISTANCE/TIME 5.75 miles (9.2km) 2h30

MAP OS Explorer 115 Exeter & Sidmouth

START Unsurfaced car park at Knowles Wood, grid ref: SY 096069

TRACKS Country lanes, pastures and woodland paths, 7 stiles

GETTING TO THE START Broadhembury is off the A373, 6 miles (9.7km) northwest of Honiton. From the M5 Junction 28 at Cullompton take the A373 towards Honiton. After about 3 miles (4.8km), pass the Keeper's Cottage pub on the right and take the next turn left, signposted to Sheldon. Continue following the Sheldon signs straight ahead for about 2 miles (3.2km) until the hill steepens and approaches woodland. Soon turn left under the barrier into the car park.

THE PUB The Drewe Arms, Broadhembury. Tel: 01404 841267; www.thedrewearms.com

8 Turn left along the edge of the field. Follow the bridleway left through the first gate, and continue back to the road. Turn left downhill to find your car.

BRANSCOMBE MAP REF SY1988

Branscombe is gorgeous. It stretches along one of the prettiest combes on the south coast, with picture-book thatched cottages – complete with roses round the door – lovely inns and an ancient church. St Winifred's dates back to just after the Norman Conquest and its tower contains a priest's room, from the time when the priest lived in the church.

Until 1987, the village bakery was the last traditional bakery in use in the county. Along with the old forge, Manor Mill and some farms and cottages, has now been preserved by the National Trust and visitors can see the large faggot-fired oven, the great dough bins and other traditional baking equipment in the baking room. The rest of the building is used as a tea room, which is up to the usual standard of the Trust. Refreshments can also be found at the beach, where the wood and thatched tea rooms have a lovely outlook, with indoor and outdoor tables.

The drive from the village to the beach is along a narrow lane that goes steeply up and then down again to the sheltered bay. Much of the land to either side, including farmland and foreshore in places, is in the care of the National Trust and there are lovely walks, including one from the village. The pebble beach has rock pools to explore at low tide and is good for swimming.

BUDLEIGH SALTERTON

MAP REF SY0682

Budleigh Salterton became a resort in the wake of royal visits to nearby Sidmouth in Georgian and Victorian times, but it was – and remains – a quiet place, free of much of the bustle and amusements often associated with seaside holidays. It occupies a position on the west side of the Otter estuary (it was originally called Ottermouth), where one of the main industries used to be salt-panning, hence the 'Salterton' part of the name.

The beach at Otterhead (the mouth of the River Otter), overlooked from the west by high red cliffs, is all pebbles, which shelve quite steeply into the sea, but swimming is safe enough in calm weather. If you prefer sand on your beach, walk westwards along the coast path to Littleham Cove, which is small, peaceful and, most importantly, sheltered from the elements.

Many fine old buildings remain in the town, including Fairlynch in Fore Street, now a small but interesting museum that has displays on local history, the natural history of the River Otter and the Budleigh Salterton Railway, as well as a beautiful display of Devon lace. The museum also has a fine costume collection. The Grade II listed building itself is of interest, being one of only a handful of thatched museums in the country, with many original features.

A little way inland is Otterton, a particularly pretty village of thatched cottages. The watermill here is the last working mill on the River Otter and you can see it in operation – milling takes place about once a fortnight. There are various displays on milling, as well as a craft shop, a gallery, a Devon food shop and a restaurant, plus live music on some evenings.

The cliffs of East Devon

This walk takes you to Branscombe along the coast path from Weston. The path has extensive sea views and passes the sloping grassy area on the cliff above Littlecombe Shoot – a popular spot for paragliders. The beach at Branscombe Mouth can become rather busy in summer, but you can always wander a little way to east or west to escape the crowds.

Route Directions

1 From the car park take the flinty track over the stile on to the footpath signposted 'Weston Mouth'. As the track descends and the sea comes into view bear left on a permissive path under trees, and follow this to meet the coast path on Weston Cliff.

2 Turn left on the coast path. Leave Weston Cliff (pass Point 8) and go through two kissing gates on Coxe's Cliff; then the path runs inland via a deep combe towards a kissing gate in the top left corner of the field. Keep round the right edge of the next field and through a kissing gate on to grassland above Littlecombe Shoot.

3 At the signpost turn half left as signed to Berry Barton. Aim for a gap in the bank ahead, bear left to a gate and kissing gate in the top corner of the next field, then turn left down the track to join the lane at Berry Barton.

4 Turn right down the lane to the Fountain Head pub. Turn right again down the valley, passing groups of thatched cottages and St Winifred's Church (right). Continue downhill past the post office and The Forge to St Branoc's Well and the village hall.

5 Turn right opposite Bucknall Close down the lane signposted 'Branscombe Mouth'. After 200yds (183m) at a path junction keep ahead through a small gate and follow the path to a footbridge (go left here for The Masons Arms). Follow the fenced path down the valley to reach the beach at Branscombe Mouth, with the Sea Shanty on your left.

6 Turn immediately right through a kissing gate to join coast path signs uphill beneath the coastguard cottages (now a private house). Go through an open gateway and left uphill to a kissing gate. Keep left up steps, then ignore all paths to left and right until, after two kissing gates and 0.5 mile (800m), a signpost points left between grassy hummocks towards the cliffs.

7 Follow the coastal footpath signs to rejoin the cliff edge, going through three kissing gates to reach Littlecombe Shoot. Retrace your steps through fields and kissing gates to regain Weston Cliff via another kissing gate.

8 Turn immediately right through a kissing gate into a wildflower meadow. Pass the cottage and outbuildings (on the right) over two stiles and on to a track leading to a tarmac lane. Go left and in a short while you'll reach Weston and your car.

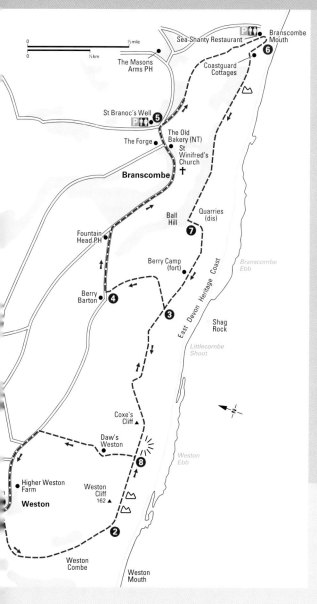

Branscombe

Sea-Shanty Restaurant
Branscombe Mouth
The Masons Arms PH
Coastguard Cottages
St Branoc's Well
The Old Bakery (NT)
The Forge
St Winifred's Church
Quarries (dis)
Ball Hill
Fountain Head PH
Berry Camp (fort)
Berry Barton
East Devon Heritage Coast
Branscombe Ebb
Shag Rock
Littlecombe Shoot
Coxe's Cliff
Daw's Weston
Weston Ebb
Higher Weston Farm
Weston Cliff 162
Weston
Weston Combe
Weston Mouth

½ mile
⅓ km

Route facts

DISTANCE/TIME 6.25 miles (10.1km) 3h30

MAP OS Explorer 115 Exeter & Sidmouth

START Unsurfaced car park at Weston, grid ref: SY 166889

TRACKS Coast path, country lanes, 3 stiles

GETTING TO THE START Weston is 4 miles (6.4km) east of Sidmouth off the A3052 towards Lyme Regis. Following signs for Weston and Branscombe, pass the Donkey Sanctuary and turn right at sign for Weston. In the centre of Weston, where the road bends sharply left at a little green, turn right into the informal car park.

THE PUB The Masons Arms, Branscombe. Tel: 01297 680300; www.masonsarms.co.uk

❶ This is an undulating walk with one steep ascent and cliff-edge paths; suitable for older, more experienced children.

EXETER MAP REF SX9292

To many people Exeter is just the place at the end of the M5, that you go past on your way to the holiday resorts of south Devon and Cornwall. But anyone who doesn't take the time to stop and explore this remarkable city is missing a real treat because it has just about everything you could wish for in a city – an important history, dating back to Roman times, magnificent old buildings, fascinating places to visit, a lively arts programme, a good shopping centre, and one or two surprises. Where else, for instance, can you explore the tunnels of a medieval water supply?

At its heart is the spectacular cathedral, which rises up from spacious lawns so that the whole building can be seen in all its glory. The earliest part, the two great towers, dates from 1110, but most of the building is of the 14th century, including the beautiful west front, with its carved figures of apostles, prophets and soldiers. Set inside the cathedral are treasures too numerous to describe in detail, but the first thing to catch the eye (and to hold it) is the roof of the central aisle. Dating from 1369, it is the longest unbroken Gothic vault in the world and can be studied using the magnifying mirrors provided.

The choir, with its magnificent oak carving, is in the centre of the cathedral. The bishop's throne, dating from 1312, is undoubtedly the finest in the country, and the 49 canopied stalls, dating from the 19th century, reflect its style. Magnificently decorated tombs and monuments, delightful features among the carvings and peaceful little chapels make the cathedral a place where you can spend as much time as you wish.

On a nice day, the Cathedral Close is a lovely place to linger, to sit on the grass or the low wall which surrounds it, but if your time is limited, don't sit for long because there is much more to see. One of the city's other major attractions is the revitalised historic quayside, where it is easy to imagine the wool-trading vessels moored up alongside the quay. Here you can discover 2,000 years of Exeter's history in the Quay House Visitor Centre, where lively displays explain the history and development of the area. Then take your time to browse around a few of the antiques and crafts shops.

Free walking tours with Red Coat Guides explore medieval Exeter, the city's maritime heritage, the Cathedral Close, and on the Ghosts and Legends tour you can learn why Exeter is reputed to be England's most haunted city.

Before bombing in the Second World War changed the city, it was essentially medieval, and a number of old timbered buildings still exist, particularly along West Street and Stepcote Hill. Exeter's Guildhall has been used as the meeting place of the council since 1330 and visitors can see its remarkable timber roof and the collection of portraits, guild crests and civic silver.

The remains of St Nicholas's Priory, off Fore Street, date back to 1070. On the special 'Living History' days 17th century daily life is recreated. A most impressive reminder of Victorian Exeter exists in the huge Royal Albert Memorial Museum, built in flamboyant Gothic style and housing rich collections.

Visit

JURASSIC COAST

Exmouth marks the end of England's first natural World Heritage Site, also known as the Jurassic Coast. Designated in 2001 on account of its fantastic geological history – covering 185 million years – the site includes 95 miles (153km) of unspoiled cliffs and beaches from Exmouth, through east Devon and Dorset, to the famous Old Harry Rocks off the Isle of Purbeck.

Insight

HONITON LACE

Honiton lace consists of small motifs, which are then attached to sheer net – even the net was handmade until the early 19th century. The craft originated when Flemish refugees came to the area in the early 16th century, and by the 17th century it was so highly prized that it was used as currency during the Jacobite rebellion. In 1840, 100 workers produced the lace for Queen Victoria's wedding dress at a cost of £1,000. More recently, a Honiton lace-maker was commissioned to produce a new jabot for the Speaker of the House of Commons. In the early 1700s there were 3,600 lace-makers in the Honiton area but lace is no longer produced commercially here today.

Visit

A BEAR'S HUT AND AN ICE HOUSE

Close to the rock garden at Killerton is a strange little house that was built in 1808. In the 1860s it became home to a pet black bear which had been brought back from Canada by Gilbert Acland. Nearby is the ice house, built around the same time. It could hold 40 tons of ice for use in the kitchen and 30 men took five days to fill it.

EXMOUTH   MAP REF SY0081

There was a medieval settlement and port here at the mouth of the River Exe, but because of the tendency to silting at this eastern side of the river, Exmouth eventually could not compete as a port with Topsham or Exeter. The docks built at the western end of the Esplanade in the mid-19th century have recently been developed and now feature a smart marina and modern housing complex, the latter enjoying superb sea views.

As a resort, Exmouth began to develop at the end of the 18th century and today it is a pleasant town and popular resort, with long sandy beaches where there are rock pools to explore at half-tide.

About 2 miles (3.2km) north is A La Ronde (National Trust), a 16-sided thatched house that was built in 1796 for spinster cousins Jane and Mary Parminter. Both the house and its contents are the result of their Grand Tour of Europe, and the interiors mirror their particular eccentricities. The rooms are arranged around an octagonal hall, and the Shell Gallery is decorated with an unusual collage of shells, feathers and other natural materials.

HONITON   MAP REF ST1600

This town is easy to explore because just about everything is in the High Street, a charming wide thoroughfare lined with Georgian buildings. Its unity of style is due to a series of fires during the 18th century, which destroyed much of the original town that had stood here since about 1200. The straightness of its main street is due to the fact that the town was originally built astride an old Roman road. High Street is one of those streets that just begs you to get out of your car and wander up and down for a while, to browse around the variety of little shops, many of them selling antiques, and explore the courtyards and alleyways that run off at right angles. The old Pannier Market, where goods were once brought from the surrounding area for sale, has now been converted into an attractive little parade of shops.

Of course, what Honiton is most famous for is lace, and there is a wonderful collection in the Allhallows Museum, housed in Honiton's oldest building, a 13th-century chapel beside St Paul's Church. The museum also has lace-making demonstrations and displays which relate to the town's pottery and lace-making industries.

KILLERTON HOUSE
MAP REF SS9700

Killerton House was built in 1778 for Sir Thomas Acland and remained the family home until it was given over to the National Trust in 1944. While the house has never been hailed as an architectural triumph, it is certainly not unattractive, particularly in its pretty garden setting, and it is a fascinating house to visit, chiefly because of the imaginative displays of its famous costume collection. Paulise de Bush accumulated more than 4,000 items of 18th- and 19th-century costume during the Second World War and around 40 original dresses at a time are displayed in appropriate room settings; these are changed annually.

The 18 acres (7ha) of landscaped gardens are the real glory of Killerton, with rare trees, shrub borders, sweeping lawns and planted beds, beyond which stretch the open park and woodland. There is a delightful rock garden, and in Killerton Clump there are traces of Iron Age earthworks. Special tourist events at Killerton include guided walks around the gardens, gardening talks and demonstrations, theatre and charity events. It is also the headquarters of the National Trust in Devon.

OTTERY ST MARY
MAP REF SX1095

This pleasant little town lies on the River Otter and was the birthplace in 1772 of the poet Samuel Taylor Coleridge, whose father was vicar of St Mary's Church. The church may seem too grand for a sleepy little Devon town, and it certainly had more modest beginnings in the 13th century, but in 1340 Bishop John de Grandisson had it enlarged, with Exeter Cathedral much in his mind. The interior is rich in medieval craftsmanship and there is an ancient astronomical clock, which is still in working order.

Not far away from Ottery is Cadhay, a classic Tudor manor house which was enlarged and remodelled in Georgian style. It is an interesting house with a history of extreme ups and downs – one minute a social honeypot, the next declining as the owners fell into debt after supporting the wrong side in the Civil War. In the 18th century a new owner raised its status once more, only for it to become a kind of boarding house for agricultural workers in the

19th century. But in 1909 Cadhay was rescued and restored and is now a fascinating and charming place to visit.

SEATON MAP REF SY2490

If you start at the Devon/Dorset border, Seaton is the first in a series of sedate resorts that stretch along this part of the coast, but was the last to give itself up to the holiday market. Not until the late 19th century did it start to expand and provide for the seaside holiday market. It lies on the west side of the estuary of the River Axe and its wide, sloping shingle beach is backed by a mixture of Victorian and more modern buildings.

One great attraction is the Seaton Tramway, with its scenic route along the River Axe as far as Colyton. Taking 25 minutes each way, the journey is by open-topped double-decker trams (or closed-in single-deckers in winter) and gives wonderful views and the chance to spot some of the abundant birdlife along the river, including swans, shelducks, oystercatchers and grey herons. Colyton, at the other end of the journey, is an attractive and historic town that is well worth exploring.

SIDMOUTH MAP REF SY1287

This is a quiet and genteel resort, and has been since it was favoured by royal patronage in the early 19th century. Much of its architecture goes back to Regency days, with elegant wrought-iron balconies and white-painted façades, and colourful gardens and floral displays enhance the scene. One of these Regency buildings, in Church Street, houses the Sid Vale Heritage Centre,

with interesting collections and detailed information about local history; guided walks depart from here two mornings a week. Visitors with a scientific bent should check out the Norman Lockyer Observatory on Salcombe Hill, with its planetarium, library, radio and weather stations, and historic telescopes.

A complete transformation comes over (or overcomes) Sidmouth during the first week in August, when singers, dancers and musicians from all over the world descend on the town for its famous festival. Organised events are staged at various venues around the town, not to mention the impromptu ones that occur whenever two or more performers find themselves in any previously peaceful pub, street corner, park or bit of beach.

UFFCULME MAP REF ST0612

This charming little village in the valley of the River Culm was once an important wool centre. Coldharbour Mill is now a working wool museum, with its original wool-making machinery, 18-foot (5.5m) waterwheel and a 1910 steam engine – a Pollit and Wigzell drop valve, horizontal, cross-compound engine, for those who know about this kind of thing. For nearly 200 years wool and worsted yarn have been produced here and visitors are able to see all stages of the production process, with guides along the way to explain what is going on.

After wandering round the mill and exhibitions you can walk by the millstream, have a picnic by the pond, enjoy a meal in the café or visit the shop.

SIDMOUTH

■ TOURIST INFORMATION CENTRES

Axminster
The Old Courthouse, Church Street. Tel: 01297 34386;
www.axminsteronline.com

Budleigh Salterton
Fore Street.
Tel: 01395 445275;
www.visitbudleigh.com

Exeter
Dix's Field. Tel: 01392 665700;
www.exeter.gov.uk

Exeter Quay House Visitor Centre
Exeter Quay.
Tel:01392 271611; www.
exeterandessentialdevon.com

Exmouth
Manor Gardens, Alexandra Terrace. Tel: 01395 222299;
www.exmouth-guide.co.uk

Honiton
Lace Walk Car Park.
Tel: 01404 43716;
www.visithoniton.com

Ottery St Mary
10b Broad Street.
Tel: 01404 813964;
www.otterytourism.org.uk

Seaton
The Underfleet Tel: 01297 21660; www.seatontic.com

Sidmouth
Ham Lane. Tel: 01395 516441;
www.visitsidmouth.co.uk

■ PLACES OF INTEREST

A La Ronde
Summer Lane, Exmouth.
Tel: 01395 265514;
www.nationaltrust.org.uk

Allhallows Museum
High Street, Honiton.
Tel: 01404 44966;
www.honitonmuseum.co.uk

Beer Quarry Caves
Quarry Lane, Beer.
Tel: 01297 680282; www.
beerquarrycaves.fsnet.co.uk

Bicton Park Botanical Gardens
East Budleigh.
Tel: 01395 568465;
www.bictongardens.co.uk

Cadhay
Ottery St Mary.
Tel: 01404 812299;
www.cadhay.org.uk

Exeter Cathedral
Cathedral Church of St Peter.
www.exeter-cathedral.org.uk

Exmouth Museum
Exeter Road.
Tel: 01395 263785;
www.devonmuseums.net

Fairlynch Museum
Fore Street, Budleigh Salterton. Tel: 01395 442666;
www.devonmuseums.net

Killerton House and Garden
(off B3181).
Tel: 01392 881345;
www.nationaltrust.org.uk

Norman Lockyer Observatory
Salcombe Hill, Sidmouth
Tel: 01395 512096;
www.normanlockyer.org

Otterton Mill
Otterton. Tel: 01395 567041;
www.ottertonmill.com

Powderham Castle
Powderham.
Tel: 01626 890243;
www.powderham.co.uk

Quay House Visitor Centre
Exeter. Tel: 01392 271611;
www.exeter.gov.uk

Royal Albert Memorial Museum
Queen Street, Exeter.
Tel: 01392 265858;
www.exeter.gov.uk.
Free.

Sid Vale Heritage Centre
Church Street, Sidmouth.
Tel: 01395 516139

Topsham Museum
25 The Strand.
Tel: 01392 873244;
www.devonmuseums.net

Underground Passages
Tel: 01392 665887;
www.exeter.gov.uk

■ FOR CHILDREN

Crealy Adventure Park
Clyst St Mary, near Exeter.
Tel: 01395 233200;
www.crealy.co.uk

Diggerland
Cullompton.
Tel: 0871 227 7007;
www.diggerland.com

Donkey Sanctuary
Sidmouth. Tel 01395 578222;
www.thedonkeysanctuary.
org.uk. Free.

Escot Fantasy Gardens
Fairmile, Honiton.
Tel: 01404 822188;
www.escot-devon.co.uk

Pecorama
Beer. Tel: 01297 21542;
www.peco-uk.com

■ **SHOPPING**
Axminster
Country market, Thu.
Exeter
Farmers' market, Thu.
Exmouth
Farmers' market, 2nd Wed.
Honiton
High Street.
Farmers' market, Fri.
Ottery St Mary
Farmers' market, 1st Fri.
Seaton
Farmers' market, 3rd Fri.
Sidmouth
Sidmouth Shopping Centre,
91 High Street.
Topsham
Darts Farm.
Tel: 01392 878200;
www.dartsfarm.co.uk
LOCAL SPECIALITIES
Cider
Green Valley Cider, Clyst St
George. www.dartsfarm.co.uk
Ice cream
The Honiton Dairy, High
Street, Tel: 01404 42075
45 flavours.
Pottery
Ark Pottery, Wiggaton, Ottery
St Mary. Tel: 01404 812628;
www.arkpottery.co.uk
Woodbury Studio Gallery,
Greenway, Woodbury.
Tel: 01395 233475; www.
timandrewsceramics.co.uk

Wine
Manstree Vineyard,
Shillingford St George.
Tel: 01392 832218;
www.boyces-manstree.co.uk
Woollens
Coldharbour Mill Working
Wool Museum, Uffculme.
Tel: 01884 840960; www.
coldharbourmill.org.uk

■ **SPORTS & ACTIVITIES**
BEACHES
Note that East Devon does
not participate in the Blue
Flag scheme.
Beer
South-facing sheltered,
pebble cove.
Branscombe
Pebble beach.
Budleigh Salterton
Littleham Cove: large
pebbles/sand.
Exmouth
Sandy Bay.
Otterton
Ladram Bay. Small, shingle
south-facing cove.
Salcombe Regis
Sloping pebble beach.
Seaton
Sloping pebble beach.
Sidmouth
Jacobs Ladder: sand/pebbles.
Town Beach: sand/pebbles.
Weston Mouth: pebbles.
BOAT TRIPS
River, coastal and sea trips
from Exmouth and Beer.
Stuart Line Cruises

Tel: 01395 222144;
www.stuartlinecruises.co.uk.
CYCLE HIRE
Exeter
Saddles & Paddles, King's
Wharf, The Quay. Tel: 01392
424241; www.sadpad.com
Exmouth
Knobblies, 107 Exeter Road.
Tel: 01395 270182;
www.knobbliesbikes.co.uk
Bikeworks. Tel: 01395 223242
HORSE-RIDING
Budleigh Salterton
Budleigh Salterton Riding
School. Tel: 01395 442035;
www.devonriding.co.uk
Exeter
Haldon Riding Stables,
Dunchideock, nr Kennford.
Tel: 01392 832645
SAILING
Axmouth
Axe Yacht Club, Axmouth
Harbour. Tel: 01297 20043;
www.axeyachtclub.co.uk
Exeter
Haven Banks Outdoor
Education Centre, 61 Haven
Road. Tel: 01392 434668;
www.haven-banks.co.uk
Exmouth
Spinnakers Sailing Centre,
Little Shelly Beach.
Tel: 01395 222551; www.
eclipse.co.uk/spinnakers
WATERSPORTS
Exmouth
Edge Watersports.
Tel: 01395 222551;
www.edgewatersports.com

Tea Rooms

The Cosy Teapot

13 Fore Street, Budleigh Salterton EX9 6NH
Tel: 01395 444016

The cries of seagulls accompany you on a visit to this traditional, genteel tea shop a few minutes' walk from the beach. Floral-patterned china, home-made cakes, a range of sandwiches and tasty lunches all add to the homely atmosphere. If you dare, try the Black Forest Cream Tea – cherry jam, clotted cream and a chocolate scone. Gluten-free options are also available.

The Southern Cross

High Street, Newton Poppleford EX10 0DU
Tel: 01395 568439;
www.southerncrossdevon. co.uk

Try this 17th-century thatched cob cottage tea room for an unforgettable experience. They have been serving cream teas with generous helpings of local clotted cream in this lovely setting for more than 50 years, and have achieved international fame. Antique tables, bone china tableware, a delightful cottage garden and even a resident ghost all ensure that tea or lunch here is a treat.

The Sea Shanty

Branscombe Beach EX12 3DP
Tel: 01297 690577;
www.theseashanty.co.uk

The thatched Sea Shanty is right on Branscombe's beach, and has been serving refreshments for more than 70 years. It's the ideal setting for a cream tea or a light lunch, with crab, lobster and fish straight off the beach. With a walled sun-trap courtyard, an open fire inside, tables by the beach and wonderful views, this is a perfect spot all year round.

Pubs

The Masons Arms

Branscombe EX12 3DJ
Tel: 01297 680300;
www.masonsarms.co.uk

This Grade II-listed inn, originally a 1360 cider house, is in pretty Branscombe. Food is serious business here: where possible, all ingredients are grown or reared locally, with lobster and crab from Branscombe beach, so expect excellent restaurant-style meals.

Double Locks

Canal Banks, Exeter EX2 6LT
Tel: 01392 256947;
www.doublelocks.co.uk

This no-nonsense pub, renowned for its good food, real ales and extensive garden, is great on a sunny day. In a cute lock-keeper's cottage on the banks of the Exeter Ship Canal, the pub is a popular choice for outdoor enthusiasts and families. The food here is reasonably priced, and has choices ranging from home-made chillis and smoked haddock fishcakes to baked potatoes.

The Passage House Inn

Ferry Road, Topsham, Exeter EX3 0JN
Tel: 01392 873653

This attractive slate-hung pub has riverside tables and fantastic views across the River Exe to Exminster Marshes RSPB reserve. Local fish is a speciality. Choose from fish pie, roasted sea bass, herb-crusted hake, a smoked fish platter and proper fish and chips.

The Digger's Rest

Woodbury Salterton, Exeter EX5 1PQ
Tel: 01395 232375;
www.diggersrest.co.uk

This dining pub has a fresh, modern decor and wonderful food made from Fairtrade and organic ingredients where possible. The menu takes in classic fish and chips, Thai green chicken curry and braised lamb shanks.

◼ NATIONAL PARKS INFORMATION

Dartmoor National Park Authority
Parke, Haytor Road, Bovey Tracey. Tel: 01626 832093; www.dartmoor-npa.gov.uk (for more information see also www.virtual lydartmoor.org.uk)

Exmoor National Park Authority
Exmoor House, Dulverton, Somerset. Tel: 01398 323665; www.exmoor-nationalpark. gov.uk

◼ OTHER INFORMATION

Devon Wildlife Trust
Cricklepit Mill, Commercial Road, Exeter.
Tel: 01392 279244; www.devonwildlifetrust.org

English Heritage
1 Waterhouse Square, 138–142 Holborn, London.
Tel: 0870 333 1181; www.english-heritage.org.uk

Forest Enterprise England
Peninsula District, Bullers Hill, Kennford, Exeter.
Tel: 01392 832262 www.forestry.gov.uk

National Trust for Devon
Killerton House, Broadclyst, Exeter. Tel: 01392 881691; www.nationaltrust.org.uk

Natural England
1 East Parade, Sheffield.
Tel: 0845 600 3078 www.naturalengland.org.uk

South West Lakes Trust
Lidn Park, Launceston, Cornwall.
Tel: 01566 771930; www.swlakestrust.org.uk

Environment Agency
Manley House, Kestrel Way, Exeter. Tel: 08708 506 506; www.environmentagency. co.uk

Beaches
Lifeguards, where indicated, are on summer service. Dogs are not allowed on several popular beaches from Easter to 1st October. For information on beaches in Devon visit www.discoverdevon.com

Coastguard
For Coastguard assistance dial 999 and ask for the Coastguard Service, which co-ordinates rescue services.

Parking
Information on parking permits and car parks in the area is available from local TICs.

Places of Interest
There will be an admission charge unless stated. We give details of just some of the facilities within the area covered by this guide. Further information can be obtained from local TICs or online.

Public Transport
Regular public transport services do not run in some of the more remote areas of

Devon. For information on transport in the county call traveline on 0871 200 2233 or go to www.traveline.org.uk

Surf Call
www.southwestsurf.info

Weather Call
Southwest weather details.
Tel: 09068 500 404

◼ ORDNANCE SURVEY MAPS

EXMOOR & NORTH COAST
Explorer Outdoor Leisure 1:25,000; Sheet 9
Landranger 1:50,000;
Sheets 180, 181

DEVON'S RURAL HEARTLAND
Explorer 1:25,000; Sheets 112, 113, 114, 126, 127
Landranger 1:50,000;
Sheets 180, 181, 190, 191, 192

DARTMOOR & TAMAR VALLEY
Explorer Outdoor Leisure 1:25,000; Sheet 28
Landranger 1:50,000;
Sheets 191, 201, 202

SOUTH COAST
Explorer 1:25,000; Sheet 110
Explorer Outdoor Leisure 1:25,000; Sheet 20
Landranger 1:50,000;
Sheets 192, 202

EXETER & EAST DEVON
Explorer 1:25,000;
Sheets 115, 116
Landranger 1:50,000;
Sheets 192, 193

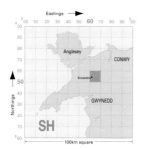

The National Grid system covers Great Britain with an imaginary network of grid squares. Each is 100km square in area and is given a unique alphabetic reference, as shown in the diagram above.

These squares are sub-divided into one hundred 10km squares, identified by vertical lines (eastings) and horizontal lines (northings). The reference for the square a feature is located within is made by adding the numbers of the two lines which cross in the bottom left corner of that square to the alphabetic reference (ignoring the small figures). The easting is quoted first. For example, SH6050.

For a 2-figure reference, the zeros are omitted, giving just SH65. In this book, we use 4-figure references, which allow us to pinpoint the feature more accurately by dividing the 10km square into one hundred 1km squares. These squares are not actually printed on the road atlas but are estimated by eye. The same process is carried out as before, giving an enhanced reference of SH6154.

Key to Atlas

M4 Motorway with number	**Toll** Toll	⏚ Abbey, cathedral or priory
Motorway service area	Road under construction	⊕ Aquarium
Motorway toll	Narrow Primary route with passing places	♜ Castle
Motorway junction with and without number	→ Steep gradient	⌒ Cave
3 Restricted motorway junctions	○×— Railway station and level crossing	♈ Country park
Motorway and junction under construction	┼┼┼┼┼ Tourist railway	County cricket ground
A3 Primary route single/dual carriageway	----- National trail	Farm or animal centre
BATH Primary route destinations	.... Forest drive	❋ Garden
Roundabout	Heritage coast	↾ Golf course
Distance in miles between symbols	Ferry route	Historic house
A1123 Other A Road single/dual carriageway	**6** Walk start point	Horse racing
B2070 B road single/dual carriageway	**1** Cycle start point	Motor racing
Unclassified road single/dual carriageway	**3** Tour start point	Museum
Road tunnel		⊕ Airport
		Ⓗ Heliport
		Windmill
		NT National Trust property

NTS National Trust for Scotland property	
Nature reserve	
★ Other place of interest	
P·R Park and Ride location	
Picnic site	
Steam centre	
Ski slope natural	
Ski slope artifical	
i Tourist Information Centre	
Viewpoint	
i Visitor or heritage centre	
Zoological or wildlife collection	
Forest Park	
National Park (England & Wales)	
National Scenic Area (Scotland)	

The Automobile Association would like to thank the following photographers and companies for their assistance in the preparation of this book.

Abbreviations for the picture credits are as follows: (t) top; (b) bottom; (l) left; (r) right; (AA) AA World Travel Library.

1 AA/Nigel Hicks; 4/5 AA/Nigel Hicks; 8t AA/Nigel Hicks; 8b AA/Caroline Jones; 9 AA/Nigel Hicks; 10t AA/Nigel Hicks; 10c AA/Nigel Hicks; 10b AA/Nigel Hicks; 11tl AA/Nigel Hicks; 11tr AA/Caroline Jones; 11b AA/Nigel Hicks; 13 AA/Nigel Hicks; 14 AA/Guy Edwardes; 18/19 AA/Nigel Hicks; 20 AA/Nigel Hicks; 21t AA/Nigel Hicks; 21b AA/Jason Ingram; 22c AA/Nigel Hicks; 22bl AA/Nigel Hicks; 22br AA/Nigel Hicks; 23t AA/Nigel Hicks; 23c AA/Nigel Hicks; 23b AA/Nigel Hicks; 26 AA/Tom Teegan; 35 AA/N Hicks; 38 AA/Nigel Hicks; 44 AA/Nigel Hicks; 46l 46/47 AA/Nigel Hicks; 48 AA; 49t AA/Nigel Hicks; 49b AA/Nigel Hicks; 50 AA/Peter Baker; 51t AA/Nigel Hicks; 51c AA/Nigel Hicks; 51b AA/R Hall; 59 AA/Nigel Hicks; 64 AA/Nigel Hicks; 66/67 AA/Andrew Lawson; 69tl AA/Nigel Hicks; 69tr AA/Peter Baker; 69b AA/Nigel Hicks; 70c AA/Nigel Hicks; 70bl AA; 70r AA/Nigel Hicks; 71t AA/Roger Moss; 71b AA/Nigel Hicks; 79 AA/Nigel Hicks; 87 AA/Nigel Hicks; 98 AA/Guy Edwardes; 100/ 101 AA/Nigel Hicks; 103t AA/Caroline Jones; 103b AA/Nigel Hicks; 104l AA/Nigel Hicks; 104cr AA/Caroline Jones; 104br AA/Caroline Jones; 105t AA/Nigel Hicks; 105c AA/Nigel Hicks; 105b AA/Nigel Hicks; 109 AA/Nigel Hicks; 116 AA/Nigel Hicks; 126 AA/Nigel Hicks; 128/129 AA/Nigel Hicks; 131tl AA/Nigel Hicks; 131tr AA/Nigel Hicks; 131b AA/Nigel Hicks; 132 AA/Andrew Lawson; 133t AA/Nigel Hicks; 133b AA/Nigel Hicks; 138 AA/Nigel Hicks; 143 AA/Nigel Hicks; 147 AA/Nigel Hicks; 151 AA/Nigel Hicks.

Every effort has been made to trace the copyright holders, and we apologise in advance for any accidental errors. We would be happy to apply the corrections in the following edition of this publication.